Computational Formalism

Leonardo

Séan Cubitt, Editor-in-Chief

The Experience Machine: Stan VanDerBeek's Movie-Drome and Expanded Cinema, Gloria Sutton, 2014

Hanan al-Cinema: Affections for the Moving Image, Laura U. Marks, 2015

Writing and Unwriting (Media) Art History: Erkki Kurenniemi in 2048, edited by Joasia Krysa and Jussi Parikka, 2015

Control: Digitality as Cultural Logic, Seb Franklin, 2015

New Tendencies: Art at the Threshold of the Information Revolution (1961–1978), Armin Medosch, 2016

Screen Ecologies: Art, Media, and the Environment in the Asia-Pacific Region, Larissa Hjorth, Sarah Pink, Kristen Sharp, and Linda Williams, 2016

Pirate Philosophy: For a Digital Posthumanities, Gary Hall, 2016

Social Media Archeology and Poetics, edited by Judy Malloy, 2016

Practicable: From Participation to Interaction in Contemporary Art, edited by Samuel Bianchini and Erik Verhagen, 2016

Machine Art in the Twentieth Century, Andreas Broeckmann, 2016

Here/There: Telepresence, Touch, and Art at the Interface, Kris Paulsen, 2017

Voicetracks: Attuning to Voice in Media and the Arts, Norie Neumark, 2017

Ecstatic Worlds: Media, Utopias, Ecologies, Janine Marchessault, 2017

Interface as Utopia: The Media Art and Activism of Fred Forest, Michael F. Leruth, 2017

Making Sense: Cognition, Computing, Art, and Embodiment, Simon Penny, 2017

Weather as Medium: Toward a Meteorological Art, Janine Randerson, 2018

Laboratory Lifestyles: The Construction of Scientific Fictions, edited by Sandra Kaji-O'Grady, Chris L. Smith, and Russell Hughes, 2018

Invisible Colors: The Arts of the Atomic Age, Gabrielle Decamous, 2018

Virtual Menageries: Animals as Mediators in Network Cultures, Jody Berland, 2019

From Fingers to Digits: An Artificial Aesthetic, Ernest Edmonds and Margaret A. Boden, 2019

MATERIAL WITNESS: Media, Forensics, Evidence, Susan Schuppli, 2020

Tactics of Interfacing: Encoding Affect in Art and Technology, Ksenia Fedorova, 2020

Giving Bodies Back to Data: Image-Makers, Bricolage, and Reinvention in Magnetic Resonance Technology, Silvia Casini, 2021

A Biography of the Pixel, Alvy Ray Smith, 2021

Living Books: Experiments in the Posthumanities, Janneke Adema, 2021

Art in the Age of Learning Machines, Sofian Audry, 2021

Design in Motion: Film Experiments at the Bauhaus, Laura Frahm, 2022

Northern Sparks: Innovation, Technology Policy, and the Arts in Canada from Expo 67 to the Internet Age, Michael Century, 2022

See http://mitpress.mit.edu for a complete list of titles in this series.

COMPUTATIONAL FORMALISM

ART HISTORY AND MACHINE LEARNING

AMANDA WASIELEWSKI

The MIT Press
Cambridge, Massachusetts
London, England

The MIT Press would like to thank the anonymous peer reviewers who provided comments on drafts of this book. The generous work of academic experts is essential for establishing the authority and quality of our publications. We acknowledge with gratitude the contributions of these otherwise uncredited readers.

This book was set in Stone by Westchester Publishing Services, Danbury, CT. Printed and bound in the United States of America.

Library of Congress Cataloging-in-Publication Data
Names: Wasielewski, Amanda, author.
Title: Computational formalism : art history and machine learning / Amanda Wasielewski.
Description: Cambridge, Massachusetts : The MIT Press, [2023] | Series: Leonardo | Includes bibliographical references and index.
Identifiers: LCCN 2022029684 (print) | LCCN 2022029685 (ebook) | ISBN 9780262545648 (paperback) | ISBN 9780262374743 (epub) | ISBN 9780262374736 (pdf)
Subjects: LCSH: Art—Historiography—Data processing. | Art—Expertising—Methodology.
Classification: LCC N380 .W37 2023 (print) | LCC N380 (ebook) | DDC 702.85—dc23/eng/20220812
LC record available at https://lccn.loc.gov/2022029684
LC ebook record available at https://lccn.loc.gov/2022029685

10 9 8 7 6 5 4 3 2

For Van and Mephi

Contents

Series Foreword

Leonardo/The International Society for the Arts, Sciences and Technology fosters transformation at the nexus of art, science, and technology because complex problems require creative solutions. The Leonardo Book Series shares these aims of artistic and scientific experimentation, and publishes books to define problems and discover solutions, to critique old knowledge and create the new.

In the early twentieth century, the arts and sciences seemed to interact instinctively. Modern art and modern poetry were automatically associated with relativity and quantum physics, as if the two were expressions of a single Zeitgeist. At the end of the Second World War, once again it seemed perfectly clear that avant-garde artists, architects, and social planners would join cyberneticists and information theorists to address the problems of the new world order and to create new ways of depicting and understanding its complexity through shared experiences of elegance and experiment. Throughout the twentieth century, the modern constantly mixed art and science.

In the twenty-first century, though, we are no longer modern but contemporary, and now the wedge between art and science that C. P. Snow saw emerging in the 1950s has turned into a culture war. Governments prefer science to arts education, yet stand accused of ignoring or manipulating science. The arts struggle to justify themselves in terms of economic or communicative efficiency that devalues their highest aspirations. And yet never before have artists, scientists, and technologists worked together so closely to create individual and collective works of cultural power and intellectual grace. Leonardo looks beyond predicting dangers and challenges, beyond even planning for the unpredictable. The series publishes books that are both timely and of enduring value—books that address the perils of our time, while also exploring new forms of beauty and understanding.

Seán Cubitt,
Editor-in-Chief, Leonardo Book Series

Acknowledgments

This book grew out of my work in the Metadata Culture research group at Stockholm University, and I am grateful for the opportunity to deepen my scholarship and explore interdisciplinary topics as a member of this group. The funding that supported this publication was provided by the Swedish Research Council as part of the project "Sharing the Visual Heritage. Metadata, reuse and interdisciplinary research" (Grant 2018-06057).

There are several individuals I would like to thank for their guidance and support. First among them is Anna Näslund Dahlgren, who has been a stalwart supporter of my research, which I have conducted over the past two years under her leadership in the project group. I would like to thank her in particular for going above and beyond to support my further development as a scholar and helping me navigate Swedish academia. Her readings of and feedback on this book have been invaluable. I am also grateful for our collaborative work and have relished the opportunity to develop projects together. I would also like to thank Karin Hansson for her feedback on my research and for our discussions and exchange of ideas over the years.

I owe a further thanks to the anonymous reviewers of both my proposal and manuscript. I appreciate the sound critique and specific suggestions that have made this a better book. In addition to these reviewers, I would also like to thank Nina Lager Vestberg for her careful reading of my manuscript and the helpful feedback she provided. Thank you also to Christina Gratorp for reading the book with an eye toward the technical details. I would also like to thank Trevor Paglen Studios for assistance in creating images, Nicolas Gonthier for allowing me to reproduce figures from his research, and Carina Popovici for taking time to answer my interview questions.

I am beyond grateful to the editors at the MIT Press for their interest in this book. I would like to thank Doug Sery and Sean Cubitt for seeing the initial potential in the project. Thanks to Noah J. Springer for guiding the book through the proposal stage and to Gabriela Bueno Gibbs for subsequent editorial work on the book.

The academic research and writing I do is made possible with the love and support of my family and friends. I would first like to thank Agri Ismail. It is hard to put into words all the ways Agri has been there for me and supported me in getting to where I am today. I wrote this book while pregnant in a pandemic and I can't imagine having gone through this challenging period without him. I would also like to thank Katie Sullivan and the extended Wasielewski family for continuing to cheer me on. This book is dedicated to Van and Mephi, who were my constant companions as I wrote it.

Introduction: Return to Form

In January 2018, an app developed by Google Arts and Culture went viral on social media, offering to answer the question, "Is your portrait in a museum?" It was the perfect hook to attract new users to a primarily educational app.[1] Combining wholesome whimsy with easy personalized participation, it quickly ascended to number one in both the Google Play and Apple App stores.[2] The viral element of the app was its "art selfie" feature, which invites the user to upload an image of their[3] face and match it with a painted portrait twin from among the works in Google's digital collection. Each pair of images appears with a percentage determination of how closely the two match. In other words, it was a classic exercise in automated image comparison using machine learning. Google billed it as "a playful way to discover art."[4] It was not long, however, before concerns began to pop up regarding user privacy. Although Google denied that the app was being used for anything other than matching faces to artworks, some online commentators nevertheless worried that it was being used to train Google's facial recognition algorithms or that Google was storing image data for future applications.[5]

For the broader public, historical artworks in major museums—as represented by Google Arts and Culture—have a largely depoliticized image. Public institutions cultivate this image of art, rightly or wrongly, to attract a large and diverse audience of visitors to their collections. In a similar way, urban developers deploy art in cities as a means of "artwashing" gentrifying neighborhoods and making them more palatable to middle-class tastes.[6] This palatability is a useful aspect of art images for artificial intelligence (AI) researchers as well, who operate in an increasingly politicized sphere. The seemingly benign use of art in such contexts means that exercises in, for instance, facial recognition may not initially raise as much suspicion as they would in other contexts. Given the implications of AI research for the field of art history and its increasing impact on art collections and institutions, however, it is vital that art historians understand and critically address how the politics of AI extend into the discipline.

"AI" is an umbrella term for contemporary digital automation methods that arrange and find patterns within the glut of data we produce. The implication of a term like AI is that intelligent machines are able to think, reason, and adapt in ways that mirror the behavior of biological organisms. However, the real-world applications of contemporary AI techniques are far more limited in scope than science fiction has conditioned us to believe. For this reason, I do not refer to the computational methods discussed in this book as AI, by and large. Instead, I speak about machine learning, a term that emphasizes the reflexive quality of contemporary algorithmic processing, and computer vision, a term that points to the pattern-recognition methods applied to images.

Art images are being analyzed in new ways that demand the scrutiny of art historians. The primary aim of this book is therefore to bring art-related computer science research back into the fold of art history. In other words, I investigate these computational studies from the perspective of art history and theory. The secondary aim is to introduce computer scientists, digital humanists, and other researchers or students actively working with computational image analysis to some of the art-historical theory and methods that may aid in understanding their work. As part of the process of developing new methods of visual analysis, researchers need to address humanistic issues and understand the historiography that their methods enter into. They can no longer ignore the mountain of criticism regarding bias in datasets and machine learning projects that social scientists and humanists have published in recent years.[7] In a broader sense, this book is motivated by a desire to reach across disciplinary divides, not in a superficial or cursory way—as is common—but by trying to bring two vastly different research paradigms into critical dialogue with one another.

MACHINE LEARNING AND COMPUTER VISION

Throughout this book, I use as little technical or mathematical language as possible to describe the computational methods in question. This should not imply that technical details are unimportant. I believe that, as new methods are applied to art historical study, it is in fact vitally important for researchers to understand the inner workings of these methods on a technical level. For an art history audience that might not have a background in computer science, however, I wanted to eliminate the barrier to the topic that technical jargon may pose. For a computer science or technically minded audience, the nuts and bolts of these methods will already be familiar but the humanistic questions around art images and machine learning may be new. In other words, my interest here is not in the efficacy/efficiency of each individual technique, or in comparisons between them, but rather in the paradigm of "viewing" that machine learning methods represent. Questions of efficacy and efficiency are already well represented in the computer science literature on this topic, which is cited throughout this book.

Any machine learning project must start with a dataset. In the case of the research profiled in this book, that means collections of art images. How these collections are assembled is thus a core factor in what automated processes will tell us about the data. As the old adage among computer programmers goes, "Garbage in, garbage out." More data is often equated with better (i.e., more accurate) results. For cultural data, however, this is not necessarily the case. There are pressing issues of bias to consider in the compilation of datasets, no matter how large they are. Construction of even the most inclusive art dataset still reflects the interests and perspective of specific cultural actors. It is important to consider who digitizes artworks and why certain artworks are chosen for digitization. For those artworks that are born digital, which works get collected or gain acceptance into the canon of high art?

Given the format of most digital image datasets, two-dimensional artworks are almost always favored. In this way, digital repositories not only reflect cultural biases but also biases of media and form. Durational artwork (video, film, sound, and performance), installation art, and three-dimensional art have made up a large part of Western and globalized art practice since the 1960s. All these forms of art are not easily represented by single two-dimensional images. Additionally, non-Western and Indigenous art may take forms that are not easily captured in a two-dimensional image. Omitting such works thus creates a historical and geographic bias and raises questions around how art is defined. Needless to say, art datasets tend to conflate art with painting.

Aside from issues of data collection, there are methodological considerations to contend with in applications of machine learning in art history. Machine learning techniques are typically characterized as either supervised or unsupervised. Supervised learning works from preexisting categories as expressed through metadata. Datasets used for supervised machine learning projects are typically divided into a training set and a testing set, and often a validation or cross-validation set. For example, if artworks in a dataset are labeled according to which artist created them, a supervised learning method might be trained to recognize visual qualities in the images associated with the labeled artist in order to automatically assign artists to a dataset of unlabeled art images. This means that we must closely scrutinize how metadata is assigned to certain images, as it is vitally important to the resulting output. Unsupervised learning, on the other hand, looks for ways to cluster or map the patterns in the data on the basis of its characteristics. This means that art images may be grouped by, for example, color or luminance. Visual form is therefore favored over other information regarding the work of art.

In order to classify or identify images, researchers develop or implement a method(s) of feature extraction/learning and classification based on one type of feature or, more commonly, a combination of features. Features are the qualities or characteristics of a digital image that a computational system can use to differentiate and sort images in the dataset. In simple terms, the visual parameters used in categorization tasks might include color, color variation, luminance, grayscale gradients and variations, identification of edges, texture, and scale/transformations.[8] All these qualities can be represented numerically via analysis of the image's pixels. They are also often represented in a type of chart called a histogram, which plots the frequency of a range of values. For those familiar with photo editing using Photoshop, the Curves editing feature is an example of a histogram. The software allows the user to see and tweak specific image parameters using this type of chart. The different features used to categorize images can be global, meaning that they are drawn from the image as a whole, or they can be local, meaning that they are based on a subdivision of the image into smaller segments.

It is worth bearing in mind that many feature detection algorithms were developed with the aim of identifying objects in an image. As with most computer vision methods, the assumed area of investigation is not primarily the digital image itself but the digital photographic image that *contains* what is of interest. This makes sense because research such as this is commonly used to perform tasks such as facial recognition or automatic recognition of road obstacles and objects for robotics applications. In order to facilitate object recognition, the feature extraction method used in the image analysis must identify points of interest and attempt to match those points of interest to see whether they are found in the same arrangement in other images.

An example of one such technique is the popular scale-invariant feature transform (SIFT) method developed by David G. Lowe and published in 1999.[9] Although SIFT has been applied to style and artist identification tasks, typically as one of several feature extraction methods, it was originally designed to address object recognition.[10] SIFT was innovative at the time of its development because it allowed users to accurately recognize and match objects within images even if the objects were scaled differently, skewed, or partially blocked.

To briefly illustrate how SIFT can be applied in object recognition tasks, I will use a series of photographs to show how an artwork (the Mona Lisa) might be identified within a gallery setting (the Louvre). Figures I.1 and I.2 show the painting from different angles, covered by bullet-proof glass and surrounded by throngs of tourists taking pictures. In these images, the painting is positioned at different distances (and therefore sizes) within the photograph, showing it from a side angle or partially blocked by arms holding up phones. SIFT can be used to identify whether each of these images contains the Mona Lisa. To do so, it isolates points of interest in the painting that can help identify whether it appears in the other photographs.

The first step in isolating these points of interest is to automatically produce versions of the reference image of different sizes that have been incrementally blurred (figure I.3). By blurring the image, the extraneous

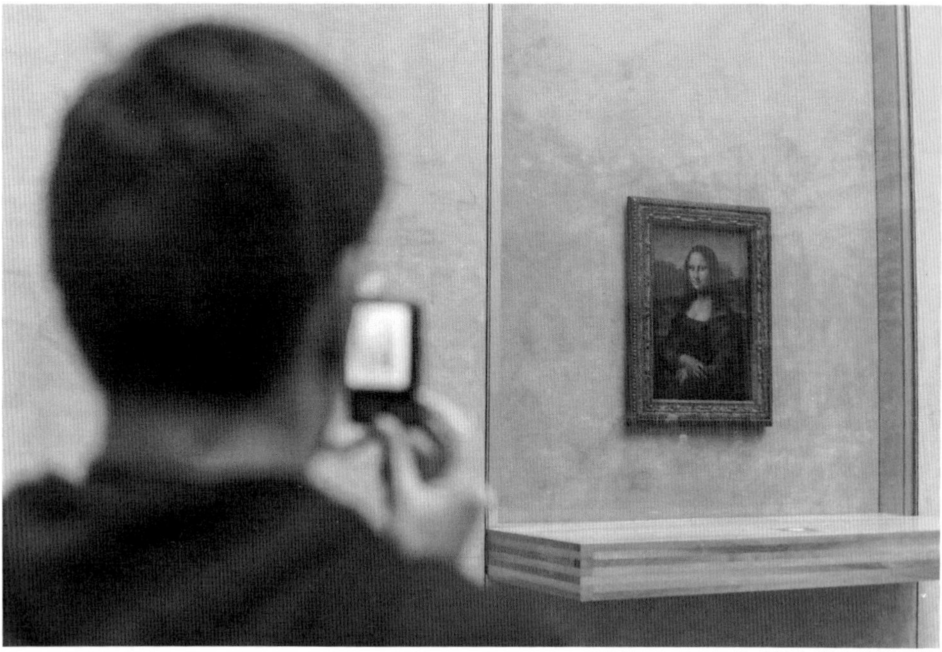

FIGURE I.1
Image of the Mona Lisa by Leonardo da Vinci (c. 1503–1506) as it is situated in the Louvre, Paris. Photo: Resul Muslu/Shutterstock.

definition, or "noise," is minimized and primary patterns in the pixels can emerge. Meanwhile, creating a so-called scale-space pyramid of differently sized images ensures that the points of interest will also not be dependent on the scale of the original reference image. The next step is to calculate the difference between pairs of these images, which also helps to identify points of interest. Following this, each pixel in each of these images is compared to its neighboring pixels, to look for those points in the image with the greatest amount of contrast or in which directional shifts in gradient can be identified.

Once these calculations and transformations have been made, the keypoints of the image can be determined and image matching tasks performed. Figures I.4 and I.5 show identified keypoints in two images of the Mona Lisa in the Louvre, and the lines connecting them show how the reference Mona Lisa can be matched to different views of the painting in the photographs of it hanging in the Louvre. There are many different

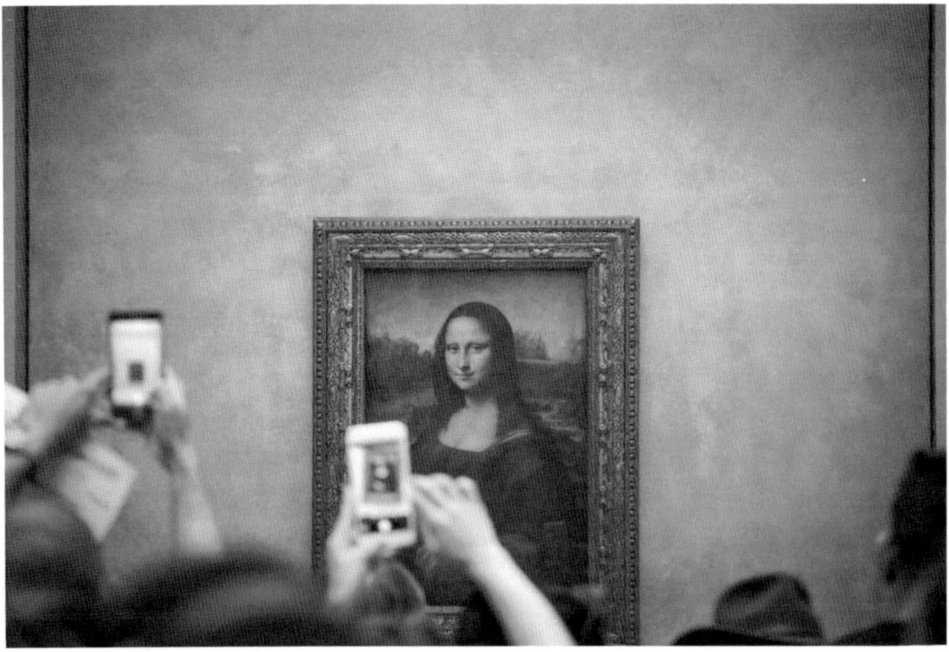

FIGURE I.2
Image of the Mona Lisa by Leonardo da Vinci as it is situated in the Louvre, Paris. Photo: SIAATH/Shutterstock.

techniques that can be used to match images or parts of images to one another. They typically identify points of interest or quintessential features of an image that help predict whether the same artist created both works.

As with SIFT, many of the other popular feature descriptors that have been applied to art image classification were developed to tackle different types of scene and object recognition tasks—none of them art classification. GIST, a method for teasing out the "gist" of the scene, was designed with the aim of categorizing the character of the scene as a whole, such as a highway or a forest, rather than individual objects.[11] In their application of GIST for art classification, computer science researchers Sergey Karayev and colleagues acknowledge that it "can represent image composition to some extent," but this was not its primary intended application.[12] Local binary patterns (LBP) techniques, on the other hand, are designed to characterize the texture pattern of the image.[13] Although the originally proposed

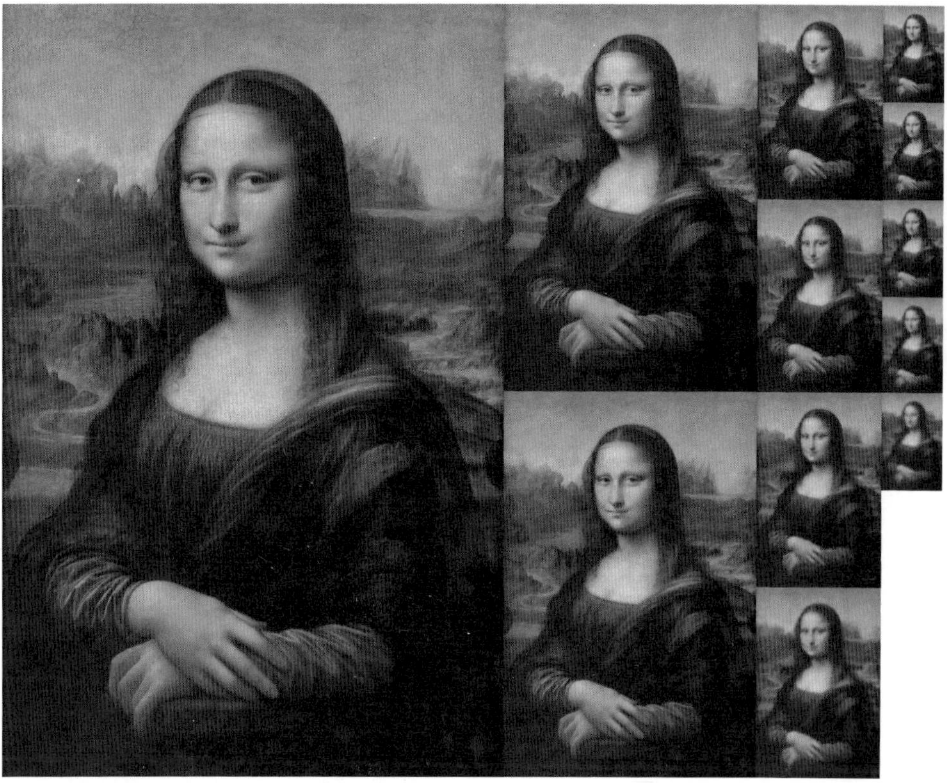

FIGURE I.3
Scale-space pyramid of image of the Mona Lisa by Leonardo da Vinci. Image: Author.

application of the technique is broader than some other feature extraction methods, its developers suggest that LBP might be used in "industrial surface inspection, remote sensing, and biomedical image analysis."[14] In another example, the proposed use for histogram of orientation gradients (HOG) was initially to help robots recognize objects and, later, to detect humans in images.[15]

Starting around the mid-2010s, research to automatically categorize art images increasingly turned away from using these traditional feature extraction methods—sometimes referred to as "handcrafted"—in favor of designing systems that would generate "learned" features.[16] One of the issues that crops up in art classification research before the uptake of deep learning was that certain features were "better" at differentiating

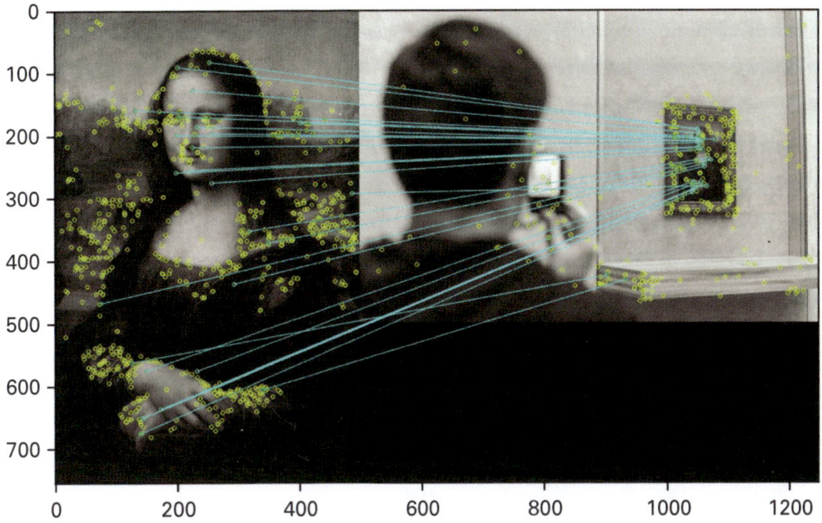

FIGURE I.4

Diagram matching keypoints in image of the Mona Lisa by Leonardo da Vinci to a photograph of the painting in the Louvre, Paris. Image: Author. Photo: Resul Muslu/Shutterstock.

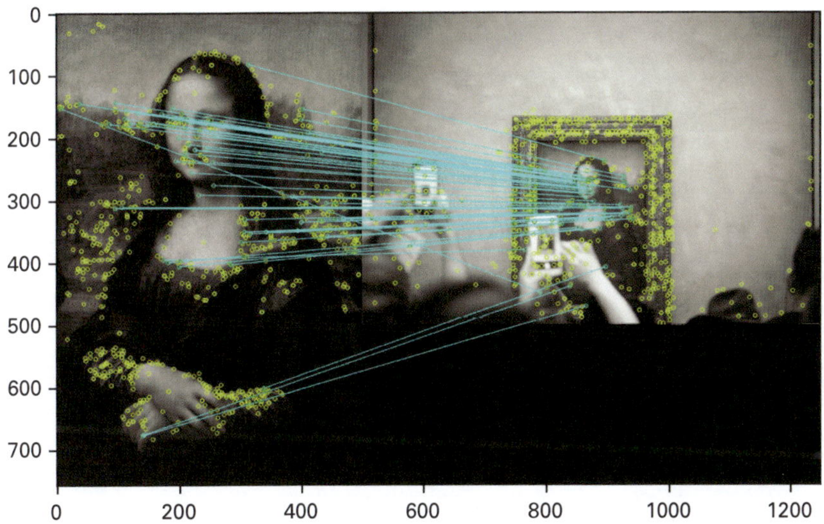

FIGURE I.5

Diagram matching keypoints in image of the Mona Lisa by Leonardo da Vinci to a photograph of the painting in the Louvre, Paris. Image: Author. Photo: SIAATH/Shutterstock.

one kind of artwork but could not be applied to other periods and styles of work as effectively. Computer scientists Hui Mao, Ming Cheung, and James She explain:

> Previous works . . . utilized handcrafted features according to some of those artistic concepts and appropriate machine learning methods to achieve automatic analysis for artworks annotation, retrieval and forgery detection. Despite the success of these works, the drawbacks are obvious: the handcrafted features are not flexible enough, it is also very hard to design a good handcrafted feature for certain task[s].[17]

As datasets grow larger and access to computational power increases, deep learning has come to dominate identification research.

The "deep" part of deep learning refers to the depth of layering in identifying features for categorization. Some of these layers identify lower-level features of the image, and these lower-level features are then used as the basis for identifying higher-level features. In other words, rather than being assigned the task of isolating a certain type of feature within the image, a deep learning system will develop features in a cumulative way, building on its initial "learnings."

This depth requires a significantly higher level of processing power than traditional machine learning feature extraction, which is one of the reasons why it has only recently seen large-scale application, despite the fact that it has been around since the 1960s. Neural networks used for deep learning are not static entities, but rather are highly variable, designed in response to the data under investigation. In the field of image analysis, deep learning really took off starting in 2012, thanks in large part to researchers Alex Krizhevsky, Ilya Sutskever, and Geoffrey E. Hinton, who won the annual ImageNet classification contest with their implementation of deep convolutional neural networks.[18]

The vast majority of machine learning and computer vision research for the classification of art images now uses neural networks. Due to their complexity and ability to automatically generate features, deep learning systems are often described as black boxes. This means that even the researchers who designed the experiment may not know how it arrives at its output. They see only what goes in and what comes out. To address this issue, researchers subsequently started devising ways to understand the inner workings of these systems through, for example, feature visualization.

For the general public and for many art historians, the field of machine learning could also be described as a black box. When computer scientists claim that they can replace art historians (or the type of analysis that art historians do) with automated processes, art historians may be inclined to believe them. However, as this book shows, art historians are in no danger of obsolescence. They may, however, soon find that their work benefits from machine learning for automated image analysis. Before new computational tools find widespread use in art history, however, we first need to overcome the academic culture war that continues to pit scientists against humanists.

THE NEW SCIENCE WARS

The rapid pace of development within machine learning research over the last decade and its application in the cultural sphere means that cultural experts and data scientists are increasingly forced to reckon with one another. Although art and science have long been positioned as opposing forces, it is worth noting that what we now call science used to be an art, in a manner of speaking.[19] That is, the study of the world before the scientific method and empiricism was quite a different practice altogether. In the nineteenth century, the study of art became a science, as early humanists adopted empirical methods. In the mid-twentieth century, the methods, standards, and overall aims of academic research in the humanities and the sciences parted ways, and the gap has continued to widen. However, digitization and quantification of cultural data is increasingly bringing them back together again.

This meeting of disparate disciplinary backgrounds has produced both enthusiastic collaboration and conflict/suspicion. An example of the former is the growing popularity of the digital humanities (DH), a hybrid field of research in which computational methods are used to analyze traditional humanities subjects. According to DH scholar Anne Helmreich, "we should understand this separation [of science and humanistic study] as culturally produced and not inevitable or irreversible."[20] There is significant resistance, however, to both the growth of digital humanities research and the use of arts and cultural material in machine learning experiments by companies such as Google.

An early example of Google's foray into the cultural sphere provides insight into the importance of productive cross-disciplinary communication. In a publication in *Science* from 2011, a group of engineers working with Google reported the results of their analysis of millions of digitized books.[21] As part of this research, they coined the term "culturomics" to describe the quantitative measurements of text and literature they performed, demonstrating how linguistic and cultural trends can be pulled from the mass of literary data at Google's disposal. The research applications of the tool they developed, Google Ngram Viewer, seemed somewhat limited at first glance.[22] For example, the authors note that "the Great War" trended during World War I and "slavery" trended during the American Civil War.[23] Digging deeper, however, the authors raise some potentially more interesting insights from the data, such as the finding that artist Marc Chagall's name was suppressed from German-language literature but not from English-language and other language literature during the early 1940s.[24] The interpretation is that, because Chagall was Jewish, German text and literature censored mentions of him. However, quantity—or, in this case, lack of quantity—is only a starting point for further research.

Some of the critiques from linguistic and literary scholars that followed the article's publication questioned the relevance of the results for humanistic research questions.[25] They also pointed out that humanists were not included in the list of authors cited, meaning that the paper largely ignored the work of established literature scholars and seemed unaware of the long-held debates around statistical and quantitative methods already ongoing in the field.[26] The fact that the lead author of the study has a background in biological systems rather than language/literature is evidenced by the contents of the paper's bibliography, in which the work of biology scholars rather than humanists takes precedent. No mention is made of any of the scholarship in literary studies, which has addressed and debated variations on these methods since the 1970s.[27] Due to the high-profile nature of the article in *Science* and the publicity it garnered in the press, it is one of the few strictly scientific papers that has caught the attention of humanities scholars. There are many more, however, that fly under the radar in non-humanities journals.

Just as the researchers in this example have taken an interest in Google's mass of literary data, researchers working in computer vision and machine learning have taken an interest in analyzing the mass of art images that have been digitized in recent years. The incursion of quantitative methods into the field of art history is too often viewed as a threat to its existence, a way in which the university pushes an increasingly neoliberal agenda.[28] Likewise, university administrations that push for interdisciplinary collaboration are often seen to do so at the expense of humanities research.[29] The reality is more complex than this.

Geoffrey Rockwell and Stéfan Sinclair, the creators of the popular digital humanities text analysis tool Voyant, predicted that the time would come when scientists venturing into the cultural sphere would have to deal with issues of method that have long occupied humanists. They write, "We suspect that the sciences, naively poaching, will find themselves bogged down in the recursive problems of interpretation that resist easy solutions, a problem that humanists have been warning others about all along."[30] That time seems to have come. Whereas "interdisciplinarity" continues to be a buzzword in academia, any communication between disciplines is often rife with epistemological misunderstandings. Merely (re-)importing scientific epistemologies into the humanities without interrogating the ways in which humanities disciplines have moved away from such paradigms over the past fifty years means that the great critiques of Western bias, structures of meaning, and universalism are all but ignored.

Despite best-faith efforts of scientists and humanists alike to bridge disciplinary gaps, miscommunications abound. Disciplines as disparate as, for example, physics and art history not only "speak different languages" and conduct research using differing methodologies, they also have more fundamental epistemic gulfs between them. The framework of knowledge that forms the backbone of a discipline is second nature to the researcher active in it but is often unclear, strange, or foreign territory for a cross-disciplinary visitor. For a researcher steeped in their own disciplinary procedures, its modes of knowledge acquisition can feel akin to a natural law.

This may partially explain why the "Science Wars" broke out between postmodern theorists and empirical scientists in the 1990s. As certain scientists became aware of poststructuralist and postmodern theory, which call into question assumptions of objectivity not only in humanistic study but in experimental science, they were keen to expose what they perceived as abuses of science and general falsehoods perpetrated by ignorant theorists. In *Higher Superstition*, for example, biologist Paul R. Gross and mathematician Norman Levitt detailed the many ways that postmodern theory had misused scientific concepts.[31] They saw contemporary theories of subjectivity as ridiculous attempts to deny the existence of scientific fact and advance a left-wing political agenda.

The most sensational episode in the battles between science and critical theory in the mid-1990s was the Sokal Hoax, in which physicist Alan Sokal submitted a spoof paper to the journal *Social Text* for a special issue titled "Science Wars." The issue was positioned as a response to concurrent criticism of postmodern theory from "conservatives" in the sciences, such as the authors of *Higher Superstition.* Culture studies scholar Andrew Ross argues in the introduction to the issue that scientists had opened up a new conservative front operating alongside the "Culture Wars," which were sparked by religious conservatives during the time.[32] Sokal was determined to show that postmodern theory was nothing but jargon-filled nonsense justifying a leftist political stance, so he wrote what he considered a paper full of total gibberish and submitted it to the journal.[33] The paper was published in the special issue and Sokal gleefully revealed his trick. The title of his follow-up book based on the incident was *Impostures intellectuelles* (Intellectual impostures), which implies that the theory it spoofs is nothing but intellectual deception and that the giants of that field—Jacques Derrida, Michel Foucault, and Roland Barthes—are total frauds.

In defense of his hoax, Sokal stated that he purposely included details in the paper that any undergraduate student of physics would understand were nonsense, if only the journal had bothered to get a physicist to read it. After the hoax was exposed, he wrote, "Evidently, the editors of *Social Text* felt comfortable publishing an article on quantum physics without bothering to consult anyone knowledgeable in the subject."[34] However, the journal countered that it was a nonrefereed cultural publication and so did not send out the paper for peer review at all, certainly not to a physicist. Given the nature of the paper, they claimed that this would not have been useful in any case as it was not a "scholarly contribution to the discipline of physics."[35]

While I was doing research for this book, I was reminded of Sokal's quote and his indignation at the fact that the journal neglected to consult a physicist on the contents of his paper. I had been trawling through countless computer science and digital humanities papers that address art-historical questions and analyze art images using only automated computational methods, and I was beginning to feel frustrated by the lack of attention or care that these papers gave to the research and theory of art historians. Surely the authors of these papers I was reading could have consulted *one* art historian in writing up their findings. Maybe then someone would have been able to point out the areas in which these scientists had misunderstood fundamental questions and concerns in the fields of art history and visual analysis. I realized that I was feeling something like what Sokal had felt but in reverse.

It is fair to say that my discomfort with much of this research is as misplaced as Sokal's in that I was not properly acknowledging the context and aims of the fields it is addressing. Even entertaining the idea that journals such as *Machine Vision and Applications* or the *International Journal of Computer Vision* would send out a paper for peer review to an art historian seems ridiculous. Many of the papers are not really concerned with analyzing art at all—at least not in the way art historians are. The majority of computer scientists seem to see art datasets as useful tools for training computer vision algorithms. For this type of research, artworks provide a straightforward problem for computers to solve. In other words, art is just another class of image data to analyze, which in turn helps hone the systems that researchers have developed to automatically recognize images of all kinds.

Unlike Sokal, who tried to use what he interpreted as the methods of poststructuralist theory and apply them to his own discipline, I address research in computer vision and machine learning using critical methods from art history. The impetus for this book was, therefore, to deal with some of these "shadow" art history research projects—to be the art historian that I wanted them to consult in the first place. As this kind of research gains a foothold in art history via the digital humanities, it is vital that computational findings are subject to the same rigor in scholarship that any other methodology would be. While we can hardly expect computer science journals to send their papers for peer review among art historians, computational methods are increasingly vying for credibility within humanities journals and so need to meet cross-disciplinary criteria. The revival of positivist methods for analyzing art images can have dire implications for society and the political landscape. For example, different forms of digital surveillance are often key applications of such techniques. By uniting some of these tools with deeper art-historical analysis, we may yet see computational methods more widely understood by the field of art history and art history better understood by computer scientists.

DIGITAL ART HISTORY

Before moving on, it is worth defining and distinguishing between the work investigated in this book and the subfield of the digital humanities concerned with art history, which has been dubbed digital art history (DAH).[36] First and foremost, this book is not a companion to or overview of current DH research and methods within art history.[37] The distinction is important to make because much of DAH research is led by trained art historians, who have a background in humanistic methods although they may choose to adopt computational ones. There is some monodirectional crossover between computer science and DAH, meaning that there are some trained computer scientists based in non-humanities departments who regularly publish their work in digital humanities journals. However, it is far rarer for trained art historians to publish in computer vision or machine learning journals.[38]

Although the use of computers for humanities research stretches back to the dawn of modern computing, DAH is a relatively new subfield of art history.[39] As such, definitions vary among researchers. Perhaps the most common way that DAH has been defined in recent years is as art-historical research that uses "computational methods," meaning those methods that process quantitative data in some kind of automated or systemic way—typically via software. One of the key proponents of this definition of digital art history is visual theorist Johanna Drucker. She differentiates between "digitized" art history, by which she means "repository building" of images and other online resources, and "digital" art history, which consists of higher-level computational methodologies. According to Drucker, "These approaches are not merely tools for accessing materials online, but ways of thinking with digital processes."[40] Some of the techniques that she cites include network analysis, visualizations, discourse analysis, virtual modeling/simulation, and structured metadata.

This type of distinction was made for digital humanities research from the inception of the term, when humanities scholars Susan Schreibman, Ray Siemens, and John Unsworth published *A Companion to Digital Humanities* in 2004. Their initial title was *A Companion to Humanities Computing*, the term commonly in use at the time. They ultimately chose "digital" instead of "digitized" to both welcome a larger audience and avoid associations with "mere" digitization projects.[41] Taking a slightly different view, engineering professor C. Richard Johnson, who works with art conservators on investigating the materials of works in museum collections, would like to once again discard the term "digital" in favor of "computational art history." He says:

> I want to imply that it's not just sorting and displaying images in large datasets, which is what is implied to me—perhaps incorrectly—by the label "digital art history." It's now much more than just managing digitized datasets. It extends to extracting information from the images, both forensic and contextual. It's modeling and simulation.[42]

Regardless of what the field is called or how broadly it is defined, the focus of DAH research is increasingly turning to image and pattern recognition techniques, the most advanced of which are the purview of computer vision and machine learning researchers today.

It is for this reason that, rather than cover the computer vision experiments conducted exclusively in the context of DAH, I wanted to go to the source of these methods. Understanding the goal and objectives underpinning the development of image recognition and computer vision methods, which often do not align with art-historical goals and objectives despite their use of art-historical imagery, can help the art-historical researchers interested in such techniques to take a critical and nuanced view of their implementation. Methods can steer a researcher's understanding of art history in subtle ways. As such, they are not merely a means to an end; they leave their imprint in the outcome of any research project.

I have also limited this study to addressing only computational methods that process images, rather than text or other types of data, and that use these methods to draw conclusions about the material under investigation. I do this in the hope that those of us writing on digital methods can get away from broader generalizations about "the digital" and discuss specific methods or groups of methods individually. Doing so may even help dissipate the use of the term "digital" as a catch-all boon or bogeyman.

Although computational text analysis can be just as formalist in nature as image analysis, there are also many ways that text and textual metadata are being used to aid the study of contextual and historical factors that contribute to our understanding of artworks and other cultural material.[43] For example, art historians Pamela Fletcher and Anne Helmreich have conducted several studies of the nineteenth-century art market using computational methods that map sales, exhibitions, and movements of artworks on the basis of textual information in digitized catalogs and inventories.[44] Once the arduous task of digitizing analogue records, inventories, and catalogs has sufficiently progressed, computational methods can be used to reveal connections and other patterns within this data.

Meanwhile, in computer science, Noa Garcia and George Vogiatzis have worked to combine art's visual and contextual qualities in deep learning experiments. They developed a system that they call ContextNet, which aims to incorporate auxiliary information alongside in-image features to better reflect the methods art historians use in the analysis of artworks.[45] This has opened up new research avenues for automated art analysis.[46] It is a promising development, from an art historian's perspective, but the type of metadata available in the experiment is still very limited. Although biases and omissions in textual and metatextual data will always be an issue, computational studies such as this are a better reflection of what automating the work of an art historian might look like in the future. Art historians regularly account for the social, political, and economic conditions around an artwork, rather than focusing on the visual appearance of artworks in isolation (i.e., their formal characteristics). The level to which such analysis can be fully automated, however, is a lingering question, and research such as that of Garcia and Vogiatzis strongly implies it as a possible (and desirable) goal.

This is not to say that pure image analysis is not useful within certain contexts. However, the results of computational techniques are not in and of themselves humanistic arguments or conclusions. This is the pivot around which some digital humanities research loses its way methodologically. Whereas humanities and computer science research may, broadly speaking, both aim to discover new "things" and produce new knowledge, the way that discoveries or knowledge are defined is very different.

There is an enormous body of literature tackling the question of how science and humanities disciplines differ and what role each plays in building collective knowledge. In my own simple terms, however, computer science research typically aims to solve problems by developing tools that automate tasks or processes that are otherwise difficult, tedious, or impossible for any individual to perform unaided and then tests their efficacy within certain quantifiable parameters. Art-historical research, on the other hand, is not in the business of solving problems.[47] Rather, it is based on interpretation and criticality. It is both retrospective and situated in its own historical context and seeks to understand *why* certain artworks, collections of artworks, or groups of artists appear, move, affect one another, and operate within societal, political, and economic contexts. In other words, for computer science, the goal may be to automate the classification and "matching" (comparison) of artworks. Once this has been done in an accurate and efficient way, the problem is solved (until someone creates a better technique). For art historians, comparison and classification are methods of interpretation; they are means by which art historians understand the *meaning* of art. Issues can arise, however, when computational methods are used to interpret the meaning of artworks without recourse to humanistic methods.

A computational technique can determine whether certain images match one another, but it cannot tell you why they match or whether the fact that they match is relevant information. There are plenty of ways that images can be compared to one another that, one could argue, are not meaningful, but the machine learning system does not know this (and sometimes the computer science researcher does not recognize this either, if the researcher is not familiar with issues of art-historical context). It is a version of the logical fallacy "correlation does not imply causation."

One example of this can be found in a project by members of the research group of computer scientist and digital art history researcher Ahmed Elgammal. In a project on automating artistic influence, Saleh and colleagues cite side-by-side examples that purport to show a relationship of influence between Frédéric Bazille's *L'atelier de Bazille* (1870) and

Norman Rockwell's *Shuffleton's Barbershop* (1950). The former is a painting by a French artist in the Impressionist circle that was created with the help of his friend Eduard Manet, who painted Bazille into the work. The latter is a popular American painting that was printed on the cover of the *Saturday Evening Post*, showing a nostalgic barbershop scene. Alongside an image on which "similar" objects and compositional elements are circled in each painting, the authors of the research write:

> The composition of both paintings is divided in a similar way. Yellow circles indicate similar objects, red lines indicate composition, and the blue square represents similar structural element. The objects seen—a fire stove, three men clustered, chairs, and window are seen in both paintings along with a similar position in the paintings. After browsing through many publications and websites, we conclude that this comparison has not been made by an art historian before.[48]

There is a reason that the comparison has not been made by art historians before: it is almost certainly an example of pseudomorphism.

This demonstrates how computational formalism, without consideration for context, can run aground. Even if it could be argued, apart from the less than compelling object relationships in the images in question, that Rockwell saw the Bazille painting and was influenced by its composition, the relationship is still not very meaningful given the vastly different context and particular signification of each work. Image similarity is not sufficient enough on its own to qualify as genuine art-historical insight. The conclusion reached by Elgammal's group is based only on the similarity in arrangement of incidental objects in the images, and it does not account for disparate motifs and themes or incorporating other archival information that might, for example, show that Rockwell had an interest in or was familiar with Bazille's work.[49]

Automated visual comparison is therefore not sufficient as a sole method for answering art-historical questions. Digital humanities research that aims to interpret and understand the meaning of culture can and must still call upon traditional humanities methods in addition to any computational methods used. If the research questions are, on the other hand, geared toward solving a particular problem or determining efficiency of different techniques, there is no need to gloss such research with humanistic methods. Confusion of purpose between the two often arises, however, as this book shows. Both digital humanists and computer scientists are tempted to draw interpretative conclusions based purely on the output of narrow computational processes. As I have argued elsewhere, however, a mixture of qualitative and quantitative methods may be more appropriate to such tasks.[50]

The idea that automated processes need to be accompanied by humanist methods in cultural research can be viewed from a purely practical perspective. There are seemingly endless debates, of varying degrees of complexity, in philosophy, computer science, and digital humanities scholarship over whether computers can think or interpret in ways that compete or compare with humans; the most famous of these is the Turing test.[51] Whereas scholars have high hopes for computers *aiding* interpretation, few seem to actually believe that computational methods can do the interpretative work. Rockwell and Sinclair, for example, call the computational methods they develop "hermeneutica," which implies that the tools themselves perform interpretive tasks. This is, however, merely a convenient elision, as the subtitle of their eponymous book makes it clear that their interpretive techniques are "computer-*assisted*" (emphasis mine). They explain that computational tools, which they consider "interpretive tools," "assist the reader to interpret the meaning of a text. . . . These tools augment reading rather than replace it."[52] The digital tool is described as something that can "bear" interpretation but not perform it.[53]

Whereas elisions in the step between computational and interpretative work are typically innocent enough, borne out a desire to impress the reader with the novelty or untapped potential of the method, it is useful to differentiate between the type of tasks machines perform versus those tasks in which the human must intercede before any results, conclusions, or arguments are published. In other words, the hype can easily outpace the reality. Machine learning methods may chart connections and uncover points of comparison among artworks that a human could never find on their own or that genuinely reveal something exciting and new for art history scholarship, but the art historian is still left to interpret it.

Even so, the use of computational methods in collaborative teams, or even by a single researcher who has multiple skill sets, need not be positioned as a pairing of opposites. From a philosophical and cultural perspective, the gulf between methods of research in the humanities and the sciences continues to widen. However, these branches of research were not always so distant from one another. One of the key ingredients in the current divide lies in the concept of objectivity.

Objectivity and Cultural Studies

All the sciences—even (or especially) the "human" ones—were originally formed around a desire to uncover universal truths based in observable evidence rather than, as academic study was previously positioned, as the result of divine design or revelation. In 1940 Erwin Panofsky, one of the foundational figures of art history, made a case for humanities study and its unique contributions. In defining the term "humanities," he discussed its origins as that which opposed both God and the natural world, writing, "Historically the word *humanitas* has had two clearly distinguishable meanings, the first arising from a contrast between man and what is less than man; the second, between man and what is more. In the first case *humanitas* means value, in the second limitation."[54] Starting in the latter half of the twentieth century, the quest for stable universals gave way to theories and systems that take into account the nuances of particular contexts or frames of reference. However, new tools for analyzing data in the humanities have resurrected a classic empiricist ideal for these fields: objectivity.

As an epistemic value, objectivity is often taken for granted in scientific fields, and computer vision and machine learning research is no exception. As the techniques from these fields migrate into humanities disciplines like art history, they bring this in-built expectation of objectivity with them. Digital humanities research, at the interface of disciplines, should be the area in which these values are problematized. However, the received assumptions of objectivity are often left unchallenged.

The conventional wisdom around big data equates more data with more accurate and trustworthy results. In simple, controlled studies, this can certainly be the case. However, big data—particularly big cultural data—is often not so straightforward. The transformation of culture to data requires a process of translation, interpretation, and representation, which is often underemphasized in quantitative cultural analysis. The implication is that one needs only to analyze and organize that data in order to draw out objective facts. Addressing the question of the representative nature of data, Drucker suggests that the use of the term "data" is a misnomer, because its etymological definition is that which is "given." Instead, she suggests that data be called "capta," meaning "taken," to acknowledge the ways in which data is "constructed" and is not "a natural representation of pre-existing fact."[55] As Drucker points out, the issue is not that quantitative analysis of large datasets or their representations cannot produce relevant research, but rather that digital humanities researchers often fail to interrogate the layers of representation that arise within such research. She writes, "At stake, as I have said before and in many contexts, is the authority of humanistic knowledge in a culture increasingly beset by quantitative approaches that operate on claims of certainty."[56] This level of certainty is rarely replicated in traditional humanities research. Indeed, one of the strengths of humanities methodologies is their self-criticality.

Over the past fifteen years, media theorist Lev Manovich has promoted a field of study he has termed cultural analytics, the use of computational methods to study culture. He sees the introduction of such methods as a way to produce generalized, mathematically grounded findings that would be impossible for an individual researcher to see, given the scale of cultural data.[57] Another goal of such research is to produce visualizations of the data that allow researchers to "see" the data en masse.[58] Manovich cites individual researcher bias and subjectivity as a key limitation for humanities research in that these subjectivities color how researchers imagine or categorize the text, images, and objects under investigation.[59]

According to Manovich, cultural analytics provides a way to reach beyond the traditional canon of art history and expand image analysis into a larger and larger visual cultural milieu.[60] He asks, "Can we think without categories?" and advocates the use of machine learning techniques: exploratory data analysis or unsupervised learning.[61] Manovich writes, "Why should we use computers to classify cultural artifacts, phenomena or activities into a small number of categories? Why not instead use computational methods to question the categories we already have, generate new ones, or create new cultural maps that relate cultural artifacts in original ways?"[62] This is also known as "distant reading," a means by which we can understand a corpus of text (or perhaps images) by analyzing the data and seeing what new findings come out of it.[63] In his book on the topic, Franco Moretti explicitly ties such techniques to investigating literature on a global scale, writing, "World literature cannot be literature, bigger; what we are already doing, just more of it. It has to be different. The *categories* have to be different."[64] This is one way that researchers have reckoned with the task of sorting through the mass of data that exists in humanities disciplines.

Claims of distance with regard to such methods, however, often take for granted that the data will mitigate rather than just collate human bias. Manovich acknowledges that data contains bias but states, "Any data project, publication, or data visualization includes some aspects of the phenomena and excludes others. So it is always 'biased.' But this is something that in most cases can be corrected."[65] I would counter that the inherent bias of data cannot be absolutely or definitively corrected. Indeed, the sheer scale of big cultural data means that sometimes biases and faults are more difficult to pinpoint precisely because of the scale of the information. Just as it is hard for a single researcher to read millions of texts, it is difficult for a singular researcher to pinpoint the bias in a large dataset. In a more recent publication, Manovich writes, "Of course, computational methods and large datasets do not automatically guarantee more objectivity and inclusion."[66] Saying as much nevertheless implies that achieving objectivity is or should be a goal of cultural studies.

Manovich argues that, on the contrary, computational methods and large datasets "help us to *confront our assumptions, biases, and stereotypes*. They allow us to notice what we otherwise may not see."[67] Data analysis can indeed yield unexpected results or provide ways to "read" many more images or texts than a single scholar is capable of reading. I have experience of this in my own research, in which computational methods helped uncover aspects of a large body of texts that I would not have been able to discover through manual analysis. In the project in question, I used text mining techniques to analyze art historical scholarship, which provided both predictable and unforeseen results.

What is at issue here and throughout this book is not that computational methods are fatally flawed or inappropriate for the study of traditional humanities subject matter, but that they are often accompanied by ideological baggage, namely, the implication that quantitative research findings are less subjective, less tied to the biases of the individual researcher employing them, and, in a larger sense, a reflection of objective conditions rather than a constructed representation of a given area, field, or object of inquiry. As Andrew G. Ferguson puts it in his book on data and policing, "Data-based systems import the biases of their builders and the larger society. Data is not blind. Data is us, just reduced to binary code."[68] Or, as Lisa Gitelman and Virginia Jackson write, "Data require our participation. Data need us."[69] Quantitative data analysis techniques are not useless for cultural studies just because data is biased. However, pretending that, through its seeming distance from our own individual subjectivities, it produces something approaching objective truth is a fantasy that has gone a long way to discredit the use of any kind of data analysis or quantitative/computational methodologies in the humanities, full stop. It is something the field must disabuse itself of, as there are always errors, uncertainties, biases, and omissions to acknowledge.

Art History and Objectivity

Scientists have long tried to distance themselves from their objects of research and demonstrate their objectivity through imaging technologies.[70] Scientific visualizations are fundamental to Lorraine Daston and Peter Galison's history of objectivity.[71] Photography played an early role—although not a deterministic one—in what Daston and Galison call mechanical objectivity, "the insistent drive to repress the willful intervention of artist-author, and to put in its stead a set of procedures that would, as it were, move nature to the page through a strict protocol, if not automatically."[72] As is the case with photography but also, more recently, machine learning, there is a tendency to read objectivity into the techniques that seem distant from one's own individual subjectivity. So data analysis and visualizations are often assumed to reveal the unbiased conclusions to be drawn from the data at hand, despite the fact that the subjectivity or bias of the source material (even if composite) remains intact.

Objectivity is not a given in science, but rather is a particular way of viewing our relationship to the world. Daston and Galison propose that objectivity arises in the mid-nineteenth century as scientific thought shifted toward finding a remedy to the flaws of individual perception and internal thought (i.e., subjectivity).[73] They write that "the fear objectivity addresses is different from and deeper than others. The threat is not external. . . . Objectivity fears subjectivity, the core self."[74] Despite its relative youthfulness as a concept, objectivity remains deeply entwined in our understanding of science, and Daston and Galison acknowledge that understanding the history of objectivity requires a leap of imagination to question what we value and take for granted in scientific research. For them, their research rendered the concept of objectivity "more specific, less obvious, more recently historical."[75] It was "a novelty so blinding as to become invisible, it came to be perceived as an inevitability rather than as an innovation."[76] This invisibility and inevitability are still reflected in contemporary appeals to the virtue that is supposedly inherent in practicing objectivity. The authors pass no judgment on the validity of the concept itself, but rather aim to open up a "debate about epistemic virtue."[77]

Daston and Galison argue that the idealized structures and forms crafted by naturalists in their atlases before the nineteenth century gave way to a moralistic imperative to objectivity, to create "blind sight" or a picture of nature free from any human interference. Once obscure terminology, "objectivity" and its partner "subjectivity" arose as prominent concepts in the nineteenth century, thanks in part to Kantian philosophy, and the modern usages of these terms spread in scientific circles.[78] It was during this time that art and science developed the oppositional relationship so familiar to us in modernism. According to Daston and Galison, "The scientific self of the mid-nineteenth century was perceived by contemporaries as diametrically opposed to the artistic self, just as scientific images were routinely contrasted to artistic ones."[79] This opposition lives on in the assumptions foregrounding debates in the digital humanities.

The quest for objectivity then turned to more basic "structural" principles, according to Daston and Galison.[80] Once images and individual sensations were understood to be faulty, thinkers searched for an even more essential form of objectivity to rally around.[81] The emphasis on physiological processes of vision and sensation that grew out of this search lives on in some of the scholarship around digital art history. For example, art historian and founding editor of the *International Journal for Digital Art History* Harald Klinke outlines a schema for art history following Panofsky that could enter into a debate straight out of the early twentieth century in its focus on perceptual apparatus:

> What Panofsky fails to describe is that before the cognitive process—which relies on cultural experience—can begin, the sensation must first be pre-processed to distinguish shades and surfaces in order to identify areas as connected objects. This requisite edge detection, contrast enhancement, and reduction of information already happens in part inside layers of the retina and the metathalamus.[82]

Klinke's use of terminology here is deliberate; the words are chosen so that we think of the eye in terms that draw a relationship between the ways in which an algorithm can be programmed to detect images and the way in which the human eye does so. The utility in forging such a connection between the human body and an automated technological process takes a page from theories on photography in the nineteenth century. The mechanical eye of the photographic camera was once seen as a means by which the precise operations of the human eye could be recreated as independent and objective.[83]

As for Panofsky, he was part of another mode of the scientific self that Daston and Galison describe: "trained judgment." The discipline of art history, as taught in universities beginning in the late nineteenth century, arose in tandem with and often relied on "trained judgment" to justify its existence.[84] Although none of the notions of the scientific self that they describe totally replaced one another, they argue that the disadvantages in interpretation and understanding of pure mechanical objectivity led scientists toward alternatives: both structural objectivity and trained judgment, "a capacity of both maker and user of atlas images to synthesize, highlight, and grasp relationships in ways that were not reducible to mechanical procedure, as in the recognition of family resemblance."[85] This belief in "the human capacity to render judgment" was applied to the scientific classification of art objects as well as scientific specimens—albeit in separate ways, and can be seen in the work of art historians like Alois Riegl and Heinrich Wölfflin in the late nineteenth and early twentieth centuries.[86] Both the scientist and the art historian of this period "entered as an expert, with a trained eye that could perceive patterns where the novice saw confusion."[87] Art history, as an academic discipline, depended on the expert's eye to categorize and typologize art objects just as the scientist might typologize human skulls, moths, or flowers. So, it could be said, that a reaction against mechanical objectivity was baked into early art history.

The art historian's insecurity in formulating a scientific discipline around the study of art could be no more evident than in the above-cited essay published in 1940 by Panofsky. Although once a giant of the field, Panofsky's work and methods have largely fallen out of favor in contemporary art history—at least until the recent interest in computational methodologies in art history.[88] Comparing the work of a "scientist" and a "humanist," Panofsky asks, "How, then, is it possible to build up art-history as a scholarly discipline, if its very objects come into being by an irrational and subjective process?"[89] He goes on to explain that the art historian has cultivated a kind of trained judgment alongside more objective processes:

> He *knows* that his cultural equipment, such as it is, would not be in harmony with that of people in another land and of a different period. He tries, therefore, to make adjustments by learning as much as he possibly can of the circumstances under which the objects of his studies were created. Not only will he collect and verify all the available factual information as to medium, condition, age, authorship, destination, etc., but he will also compare the works with others of its class, and will examine such writings as reflect the aesthetic standards of its country and age, in order to achieve a more 'objective' appraisal of its quality. . . . Thus, what the art-historian, as opposed to the "naïve" art lover, does, is not to erect a rational superstructure on an irrational foundation, but to *develop* his re-creative experiences so as to conform with the results of his archaeological research, while continually checking the results of archaeological research against the evidence of his re-creative experiences.[90]

This leads, in Panofsky's conception of the discipline of art history, to a kind of humanistic objectivity, led by the categorizing power of the subjective trained expert. He did this primarily by performing meticulous iconographic studies of "classes" or "typologies" of works of art. Needless to say, in Panofsky's time, very few art historians were looking with a historical perspective on modern art (i.e., nineteenth- and early twentieth-century art). So Panofsky's assumption of "archaeological" study as an essential component of "art historical" study in this essay would not have been treated as disciplinarily discrete, as it often is today.[91]

Alongside new digital tools for analyzing images, a resurgent mechanical objectivity has arisen: an objectivity that promises that machines can also exercise trained judgment. In light of this, the methods of figures like Riegl, Wölfflin, and Aby Warburg have been dusted off after long periods of dormancy in the field. It is no accident that Warburg called his life's work an *atlas* (the Mnemosyne Atlas) because his working methods took their cues from the assembly of atlases in the natural sciences, such as the ones described by Daston and Galison. With the advent of new digital tools to perform pattern recognition on image databases, however, the area of trained judgment is now seen as something that can be replaced by a *mechanically objective* trained judgment. Researchers using computational methods have been working to create systems that delegate trained judgment—once the exclusive domain of the human subject—to automated systems. So, with the possibility that trained judgment can be automated, we return to questions of mechanical objectivity and scientific reliance on it as an ideal.

Among those unfamiliar with humanities methods, there is a common misconception that humanities research is comparable to personal reflection or artistic research and proceeds from the humanist themself rather than from the object of inquiry. However, rather than personal reflections based on individual sensations, academic research in the humanities actually errs toward considerations of the external and, as such, aims to remain uncompromised by lack of evidence or researcher bias. Distanced analysis, commentary, and observations on a research subject—something approaching the ideal of objectivity—is a standard practice in art historical research, as in other humanities disciplines. So, objectivity is not an epistemic virtue to be dismissed outright as flawed or compromised by its history. Unfounded idealistic claims of objectivity for humanities data or the categories and output of that data, however, do not aid in the investigation of art-historical topics. Given the stakes and complications involved, we might as well rule out objectivity as a goal of art history. This presents a problem for data-driven research that fails to account for possible biases in art-historical datasets.

If objectivity is the implicit epistemic value underlying mathematically oriented research methods, then the research object itself must have a stable meaning or composition that can be measured and compared to other similar research objects. Social, cultural, and contextual factors that might contribute to the meaning of a work of art are not only difficult to quantify, but they also have different quantitative parameters from a typical art object and are therefore difficult to mathematically peg to those of the artwork. This means that both contemporary computational research and earlier art-historical research have focused on the formal characteristics of the work of art and the meaning inherent in analyzing the properties of form over externalities. The concreteness of form, however, does not mean that its meaning is equally concrete.

Computational Formalism

Form is the essence of a work of art, but it is also highly ambiguous. It is an artwork's visual and material properties or its compositional elements (i.e., its superficial appearance), but it also contains an artwork's effervescent quality, its expressive power. Form is familiar and alien at the same time and can seem to evolve of its own volition. Art history has, over the years, concerned itself with how form, in its open-ended manifestations, both produces and inhabits the intellectual, cultural, and personal milieus of its creators. Some scholars believe that art has its *own* history, driven internally by an evolutionary impulse in form itself.[92] Form on its own, however, is merely a collection of interrelated features. Art historians are tasked with understanding how the meaning of a work of art is expressed through these features.

Many of the founders of art history took taxonomy as their prime objective and formalism was the means by which they pursued it. They pitted themselves against those who, in their view, debased art and aesthetics through historical determinism, that is, those who saw art as merely a product of its time.[93] Whereas in the past art historians were primarily concerned with ordering art objects according to their formal qualities, like naturalists charting the relationships between different species of flower, the discipline has subsequently widened its concerns. Rather than part of a history of style, typological study, or even Kublerian "network," the form an artwork takes is now typically assumed to relate to *something* outside of it: the cultural, social, or political context; a greater metaphor; or the reception of the work via its use, experience, or viewership.[94]

Formalism has thus developed "a bad name" in art history, as it is seen to prop up dominant power structures and biases.[95] In light of this, some art historians have sought to unravel the foundational relationship between formalism and the study of art history. David Summers, for example, has issued extensive critiques of the practice of formalism and its connection to nineteenth-century metaphysics.[96] Summers argues for what he calls a post-formalist art history that does not rely on visual perception as the epistemological basis of the discipline.[97] Nevertheless, formalism remains a core method in art history. When the physical, visual, or material properties of a work of art are an essential part of a scholar's argument, the method must be described as at least partially formalist.

Art historians who still define themselves primarily as formalists can no longer escape discussing the social or political aspects of art, however. Often enough, to do so is quite undesirable. The idea that art should remain purely self-referential or autonomous is nothing other than a "silly dream," as one of the discipline's most high-profile formalists, Yve-Alain Bois, terms it. Forced to point out the obvious, he declares, "it is impossible to keep meaning at bay."[98] As critical theory perspectives have come to dominate the discipline of art history, purely formalist analysis has gradually disappeared. Taxonomy is no longer the primary interest of the field.

The transitional period for this change began in the 1960s and early 1970s with the arrival of the "new" art history, a set of methodologies and critical perspectives that addressed the political and ideological dimensions of art.[99] This was a version of art history that followed in the wake of the early and influential art historian Meyer Schapiro, who united the concept of style with social and political concerns starting in the 1930s. He writes,

> By considering the succession of works in time and space and by matching variations of style with historical events and with the varying features of other fields of culture, the historian of art attempts, with the help of common-sense psychology and social theory, to account for the changes of style or specific traits.[100]

Critical perspectives in art history began their rapid rise in dominance in the late 1960s, while taxonomy, iconography, and connoisseurship slowly faded to the background.

Written at the height of this transitional period between the old and the new art history, W. Eugene Kleinbauer's 1971 work of art historiography,

Modern Perspectives in Western Art History, divides the field's methodologies into "intrinsic" and "extrinsic." This divide could otherwise be termed formalist and nonformalist:

> Intrinsic perspectives focus on describing and analyzing the inherent qualities of the work of art. They deal with materials and technique; problems of authorship, authenticity, dating, and provenance; formal and symbolic characteristics, and function. In other words, they proceed from the work of art itself and aim to delineate its properties. Many scholars hold that art historical inquiry should be limited to these matters, and they restrict their investigations accordingly. Others maintain that a full understanding of the work of art requires an examination of the various conditions surrounding and influencing it.[101]

Surveying the field fifty years later, it is evident that the situation described by Kleinbauer is somewhat reversed. Many scholars in art history today hold that art-historical inquiry should always incorporate extrinsic perspectives. Few, as evidenced by Yves-Alain Bois's statements quoted above, could credibly restrict their investigations to merely intrinsic perspectives without attracting criticism that their methods are outdated and irrelevant.[102] However, the recent rise of computational methodologies in art history has ushered in a renewed interest in research based on mass formal comparison.[103]

In this book, I have coined the term "computational formalism" to describe this methodological development, defining it as a revival of formalist methods in art history facilitated by digital computing. What are the implications of this shift back to formalism within art history? Computational formalism is, in many ways, very similar to traditional formalism: it analyzes the external features/qualities of the work, often to the exclusion of contextual factors; it is based on comparison; and its aim is to create systems of classification and taxonomy for artworks. However, computational formalism differs in fundamental ways from human/manual formalism. One of the key ways, as mentioned, is that it gives researchers the ability to analyze large amounts of data in a relatively short time. Another way that it differs, however, is in the type of features and measurements that computational systems make in order to compare artworks.

A case from literary studies, in which the authors developed methods that they term "quantitative formalism," illustrates this last point and demonstrates the extent to which computational formalism may differ from traditional formalist methods, even if the findings are the same as or similar to human formalist analysis. Literary scholars Sarah Allison, Ryan Heuser, Matthew Jockers, Franco Moretti, and Michael Whitmore began a study in 2008 in which they used a text-tagging tool called Docuscope to comb through a corpus of texts in different genres and sort them in an unsupervised manner.[104] The initial results of their studies astonished them. The computational methods they used were able to match already established genre groupings with a high degree of accuracy.

On closer inspection of the material, however, they found that in order to indicate each text's genre, Docuscope was identifying wording and word combinations that were completely different from those that a human would use. Investigating a single page that was isolated as the most "gothic" in the corpus, they write, "For us, that page was gothic because of the subdued terror and the archway, the ruin and apprehension and the limbs that trembled—not because of the *he, him, his, had, was, struck the,* and *heard the* which caught Docuscope's attention."[105] Furthermore, they found that Docuscope had a hard time isolating genre as opposed to author owing to the focus on minute elements of language rather than overarching plot points. In other words, although the methods of both human and computer are formalist, the formal elements that they isolate tend to be extremely different.

This is also true for computational formalism as applied to images. How computers "see" images is fundamentally different from how humans process image data. As in the example above from literary studies, computational formalism in image analysis typically isolates or pinpoints units that are more basic and granular—the fundamental building blocks rather than the overall impression. As Allison and colleagues write, "Genres, like buildings, possess distinctive features at every possible scale of analysis: mortar, bricks, and architecture, as Ryan Heuser put it: the mortar, the grains of sand, of Most Frequent Words, the bricks of Docuscope's lexicogrammatical categories, and the architecture of themes and episodes that readers recognize."[106] Whereas dataset bias is the most common point of critique for contemporary machine learning applications, recent research has also pointed to the need to account for internal algorithmic bias, or what Fabian Offert and Peter Bell call "perceptual bias."[107] In their paper, they investigate the granular elements—or features—of an image that convolutional neural networks fixate on. Feature visualizations are a type of composite image that exposes or reveals the features of the image that the computational system has isolated as key to its categorization efforts (for example, color variation, luminance, gradients, edges/line, texture, and scale/transformations), much like the words *he, him, his, had, was, struck the,* and *heard the* in the foregoing example. Unsurprisingly, the "perceptual topology" of these automated image "viewers" is very different from that of human viewers. On the basis of this difference, we can extrapolate that the paradigms of formalism for the human and for the machine learning system are disparate as well. Hence, computational formalism bears a relationship to historical methods of formalism, but it shifts the focus to radically different formal elements.

This is an example of how one might find bias in unsupervised machine learning experiments. Although the images are not "labeled" problematically, there is still bias that is based on what features the algorithm latches onto as defining a particular subset of images. An understanding of this different way of "seeing" is absolutely essential as researchers continue to use and develop machine learning techniques.[108] Although traditional and computational formalism share a basic focus on the external appearance of a work of art, they go about the task in disparate ways. The "thought processes" of machine learning systems are often opaque to the researchers using them, which presents a problem for humanists interested in methodological self-criticality. Understanding not only data bias but also perceptual bias will help humanists maintain a level of self-criticality in their methods, especially if those methods are computational.

QUESTIONS OF STYLE

This book explores how the computational formalist methods of computer vision and machine learning today mirror or relate to traditional formalist methods in the discipline of art history. For both old and new formalisms, categorization and analysis by style is of paramount importance. In simple terms, style can be defined as the distinctive manner in which an object is made, as identified by certain formal characteristics.

This distinctiveness, of course, can be identified only in comparison to other distinctive manners of making, implying that style is a highly relative quality. It is therefore an unstable and slippery foundation upon which to peg mathematical "certainty."

Although these two interrelated terms—form and style—are easily conflated, they differ in subtle ways.[109] According to two art historians, Whitney Davis and Richard Neer, stylistic analysis indicates a *cause* for the particular arrangement or formal configuration of a work.[110] As Davis writes, "What formalism identifies as formed (or configured) will be specified in stylistic analysis as made (and sometimes deliberately stylized) by a particular agent who can be identified by that style."[111] Stylistic analysis as indicative of causality, whether the method is automated or manual, forms the basis for my analysis of computational methods in this book.

Following Wölfflin's conception of the "double" nature of style, Richard Wollheim writes that, in discussions of art, "the concept of style is disposed to turn up twice. Sometimes we think about and talk of *general style*: sometimes we think about and talk of *individual style*."[112] This means, broadly speaking, that style can either mean a grouping of formally similar works, whether or not they are from a particular time period (e.g., naturalism, impressionism, or baroque), or it can mean a grouping of works attributed to an individual artist based on their formal characteristics (e.g., the style of Rembrandt or even the style of an unnamed yet recognizable individual artisan). These two conceptions of style also roughly describe the division of this book: chapter 1 is largely confined to issues of general style, whereas chapter 2 focuses mainly on individual style. This is not the only way in which the division of this book can be described, however. Chapter 1 focuses primarily on data and dataset creation/organization, and chapter 2 discusses machine learning methods, particularly the use of deep learning in recent years, and their implementation.

Flowing from the focus on general style, chapter 1 addresses the art-historical data that is used in computer vision and machine learning research, questioning how it is constructed and what biases may be inherent in implementing automatic style categorization based on the art datasets that researchers currently have at their disposal. In essence, this chapter addresses digitization, selection, and categorization of datasets in art history. Before any sophisticated machine learning method is applied to a dataset, it goes through a process of curation and creation. The composition and how that composition affects the output of a process are often taken for granted, although the composition is fundamental to the results of any machine learning experiment. It is certainly possible to incorporate work beyond the traditional western canon of art in computational image analysis, but the reality is that the canon has been given preference in institutional digitization projects and so is often the only digitized work with complete metadata that is available to researchers. Canonical datasets of artworks therefore tend to be used and reused in art-based computer vision and machine learning projects, which uncritically reproduce the biases contained therein.

Chapter 2 moves beyond discussion of data and its biases to address methods of artwork attribution, both computational and traditional (i.e., connoisseurship). Machine learning methods are increasingly being deployed for both art identification and authentication tasks. On one hand, identification may mean isolating and naming content or objects *within* an image. Such procedures can be highly useful to researchers at the beginning stages of research, as a means by which to streamline the process of searching large image collections or understanding documentary images with little attendant metadata. Identification can also relate to determining the artist who created a work, which has direct implications for the art market. Attendant to this, tech start-ups that use deep learning to determine the authenticity of artworks are beginning to emerge. However, the concurrent rise of creative deep learning techniques, such as generative adversarial networks, promises to produce compelling "new" artworks from long-dead artists. "Deepfake" videos, which use deep learning to create seamless fakes of, for example, public figures engaged in controversial or illicit activities, have been proliferating in recent times, but works that could be termed deepfake artworks already exist. Although the "fakes" I profile in this chapter are not intended to fool anyone, more nefarious fakes may lie just over the horizon, as creative algorithmic methods and printing techniques improve.

Computational image recognition, sorting, categorization, identification, and creation techniques have increasingly become a part of daily life for many people around the world, whether they are consciously used or more covertly applied. Applications range from the sinister, such as state and commercial surveillance, to the mundane, such as automated photo sorting by mobile phone software. For those who deal with the theory and understanding of images (i.e., art historians and visual theorists), machine learning techniques continue to increase in use and relevance and will likely soon be applied to most major image collections of art and other visual material in some way. Such techniques have the potential to significantly aid researchers in their work, but they are not a panacea for perceived weaknesses in humanistic study, namely, the lack of objectivity or dispassionate empiricism.

This book critically examines the strengths and weaknesses of machine learning as applied to art history. In doing so, I do not wish to reject such methods of image analysis outright nor to celebrate them as an unequivocal improvement in how research is conducted in the discipline. Rather, in opening up an interdisciplinary dialogue between computer science and art history, the aim is to move beyond superficial or one-sided collaboration to something approaching understanding, both for theory and for practice.

1

The Shape of Data

In the title of their 2017 paper, Loris Nanni and Stefano Ghidoni ask, "How could a subcellular image, or a painting by Van Gogh, be similar to a great white shark or to a pizza?"[1] Strangely enough, the study of art history up to this point has been little concerned with how similar Van Gogh's paintings are to pizza or sharks. In computer vision and machine learning research, however, all sorts of disparate images are regularly compared. Human art historians, who have learned to distinguish image content over a lifetime, already know the difference between images of pizza and images of sharks at the start of their art history training. Computational systems, however, do not "learn" in the same way. In the case of this particular article, pizza and sharks are just a sampling of the content found in twenty-one different image datasets that the researchers used, which include everything from pictures of smoke to hamster ovaries to Brazilian flora. This variety of image data was gathered in order to tackle the question of whether image recognition in particular categories can be improved by past learning from images that have been sorted by a variety of parameters. This is something called deep transfer learning. In short, can training an algorithm to detect a great white shark help it later identify a Van Gogh painting?

In order to recognize different parameters and automatically classify a particular image or elements within them, researchers need images to train the system (a training set) and to test the effectiveness of the system (a test set). A training set is usually a representative portion of the latter that is then excluded in testing the system.[2] Nanni and Ghidoni's study is but one example of this kind of research. There are many other pieces of research that have a narrower focus and concern themselves only with categorizing images of artworks. Datasets often get recycled in computer vision and machine learning research. In this study, the authors use one such preexisting art history dataset, Painting-91, as part of a compilation of image datasets.[3]

In recent years, smaller datasets used to categorize artworks, such as Painting-91, have increasingly been replaced by larger repositories with many more images and more extensive metadata, such as WikiArt. Nevertheless, copyright remains a significant barrier to amassing large datasets of images.[4] The metadata for these datasets, which is crucial for stylistic labeling, are either crowdsourced from the general public or, as with the case of digitized museum catalogs, labeled by art historians or volunteers with some art-historical expertise. In order to understand computational formalism as a part of the longer trajectory of art-historical formalism, we need to first look at how style is defined via some of these datasets. Since they are reused over and over again by different researchers, whatever internal issues they might have are spread throughout the field of computational image analysis.

Computer science research moves fast, and the techniques used to identify the content of art images have rapidly advanced in the past ten to fifteen years. Computer vision, machine learning, and related fields have taken up the task of automating human vision's capacity to identify images (or elements of images) on the basis of the arrangement of texture, color, shape, and line within them—their formal qualities, to put it in art-historical terms. It is distinctive from the methods used for image retrieval in most standard art databases, which are still based on keywords or textual metadata rather than analysis of the images themselves. The rise in machine learning techniques has made a different kind of image retrieval and identification possible in that computational systems can now make new connections that are not preprogrammed but that are based on learning from "looking" at a large number of images. Computers are increasingly able to extrapolate patterns based on what they have "seen" before and successfully identify images that they have never previously encountered. Generative techniques such as generative adversarial networks (GANs) have even been used to create new images on the basis of what the system has extrapolated from existing databases of artworks.[5]

This chapter provides a detailed analysis of recent computer vision and machine learning research that specifically deals with categorization of art images by period or movement style (henceforth referred to merely as "style"). Although style was once an important subject of theory and debate in art history, its prominence as a scholarly concern declined significantly during the latter half of the twentieth century as critical theory methods, which question scholarly bias and the erasure of contextual power relationships, rose in importance. However, the recent quantitative turn in art history and other humanities fields has renewed interest in taxonomical and formalist concerns, including questions of style. In what follows, I investigate the use of art datasets in order to understand how style has been framed by computer science in recent years. The aim in doing so is not to critique the computational and mathematical work done by computer science researchers. I take it as a given that automated systems will become better and better at recognizing image content that reflects the properties of digital images. The main purpose is rather to question the assumptions that quantitative researchers make when they employ stylistic categories through computational means, designing automated art sorting systems that are based on the formal properties of digitized artworks. I explore the input into the system, that is, the datasets on which computational systems are trained, in order to understand the ways in which style is (re)conceived through new automated formalist methods.

The appendix details the scope of the research that I survey in this chapter in a comprehensive and condensed way, exploring a fifteen-year trajectory in image categorization and art dataset creation within the fields of computer vision and machine learning. An overview such as this would not typically appear in computer science literature, because categories such as style and authentication are assumed to be objective and established. From an art-historical point of view, however, separating these metrics is essential to understanding and interpreting the results of these studies. This in-depth analysis begins with a discussion of the goals of computer science research with regard to art images, namely, training computational systems to identify higher level semantic categories such as style and automating some of the tasks performed by human art historians. I then discuss common issues within art image datasets: how images are selected and presorted. I argue that datasets typically perpetuate a traditional, Western-centric canon of art history and that issues of power and representation are often unaddressed in the creation of experimental datasets. Even as datasets grow in size to encompass ever larger collections of images sourced from established museums, these biases persist unremarked. One of the key issues I highlight in this section of the book is how contextual issues in art history are discarded in favor of purely formalist analysis. Style, therefore, is often assumed to have a one-to-one relationship with the visual characteristics of a work of art.

DIGITIZATION AND DATASET CREATION

Since the 1980s, art historians have worked to digitize slide libraries in universities and to either create digital photographs or digitize existing photographs of items in museum collections.[6] This has been quite a long process, often limited by lack of technical knowledge and financial constraints within institutions. In my own experience, the uptake of even basic digital tools in the field of art history has been slow and idiosyncratic. When I was an undergraduate student circa 2004, the transition from slides to digital images was still underway at Northwestern University's art history department. Whereas some faculty members were involved in cutting-edge digital projects, such as a Mellon-funded initiative to create 360-degree interactive photo documentation of Buddhist paintings in the caves of Dunhuang, others had no idea how to use PowerPoint and were still relying on two slide projectors for their lectures.[7] By 2012, when I began my doctoral work, the digitization of the art history slide library at the Graduate Center at the City University of New York had been completed, and the department was paying students to digitize images scanned from books into a private database rather than subscribe to the art image database ArtStor. I wondered how many other departments were replicating the same image repositories.

Until fairly recently, the segmentation and proprietary nature of most digitization projects within art history has limited their use by computer scientists. Museum image databases are increasingly available to the general public, but many are still accessible only for museum staff or within museum research libraries. The back end of museum databases and attendant metadata are rarely released directly to the general public. Given the restrictive nature of most digitized art repositories, it is unsurprising that computer vision papers prior to 2015 dealing with art images often relied on bespoke datasets created by computer scientists, sometimes in collaboration with existing museums or collections but often simply gathered from "the internet."

One of the most concerning and highly critiqued aspects of contemporary image dataset collection and sorting procedures is the replication of human bias under the guise of objective categorization. On a basic level, this is a metadata issue because it has to do with how training sets—the datasets used to train machine learning algorithms how to look at images—have been labeled or categorized by humans. For art history, image selection (i.e., what is included in the canon of art history) has long been problematic. It is also an issue of black box machine learning, meaning that researchers have no idea why a particular algorithm makes the "decisions" it makes because they can see only the input and output from the system.[8]

In annotating large-scale image collections, the vast majority of machine learning systems generate tags for "content"/motif, that is, what is depicted—a bird, a car, a man with a hat, and so on. Although this type of label may be useful for certain applications such as detecting people and things in surveillance footage or training a self-driving car to recognize road hazards, it is often not very useful for academic researchers.[9] The metadata for many image collections is created using human crowdsourcing, but researchers are increasingly interested in creating tags automatically via machine learning techniques.[10] Although some computer science researchers are beginning to recognize the need to investigate bias in machine learning systems, the assumption is still often that these categories are objective or unchanging—once the "right" categories have been determined. Surapaneni and colleagues, for example, acknowledge the need to redress bias in their experiments with the Metropolitan Museum of Art's image collection, though their work focuses primarily on image content rather than other categories.[11]

Bias in machine learning and algorithmic systems has been profiled in numerous publications over the last several years, which show how datasets tend to replicate and even exaggerate biases inherent in our societies.[12] One project by researcher Kate Crawford and artist Trevor Paglen profiled the absurdity as well as the darker implications of bias in the ImageNet database, which they call "the most iconic training set of all."[13] This popular database was specifically designed for computer vision and object recognition research and was created by hand-tagging images on the basis of the "objects" that they contain, a task that was performed by low-paid humans using Amazon's Mechanical Turk, a digital piecework system.[14]

In addition to publishing an essay detailing their "excavation" of this dataset online, Crawford and Paglen created a viral tool called ImageNet Roulette, with which anyone could upload a picture and see what kind of strange assumptions might be superimposed on seemingly innocuous scenes or people.[15] The results were both humorous and troubling. Rather than reproduce some of the racist and misogynist results that went viral along with the project, which can still be readily found online, I input an art-historical image, *The Anatomy Lesson of Dr. Nicolaes Tulp* (1632) by Rembrandt, into ImageNet Roulette. As figures 1.1 and 1.2 show, the categories that the system assigned to the men in the painting are highly absurd.

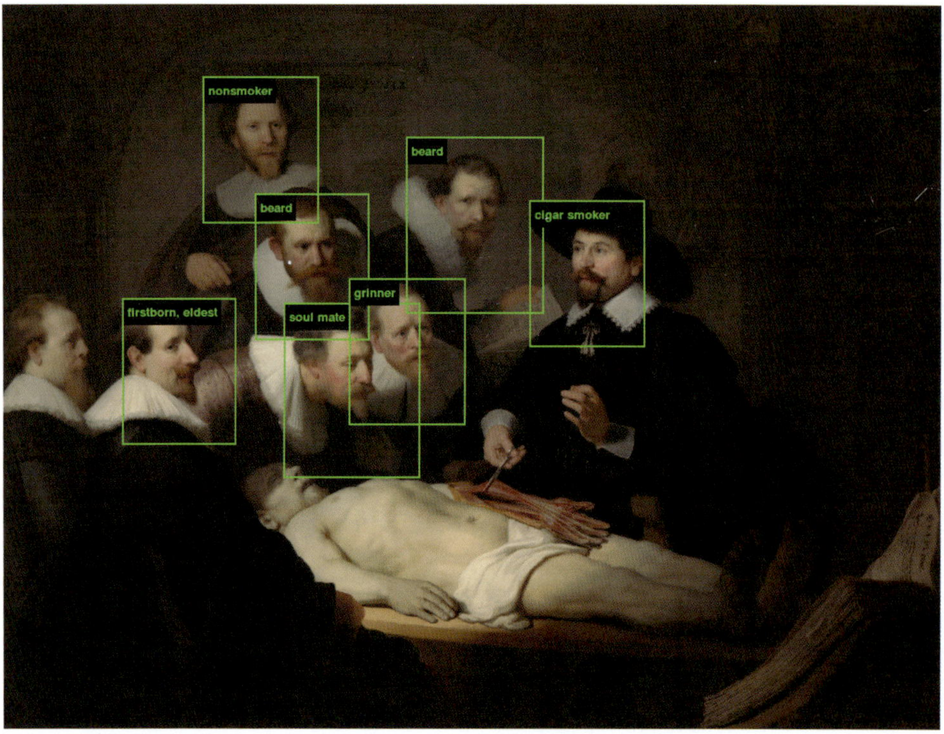

FIGURE 1.1
ImageNet Roulette results based on image of Rembrandt van Rijn's *The Anatomy Lesson of Dr. Nicolaes Tulp* (1632). Image: Author, with permission of Trevor Paglen Studio.

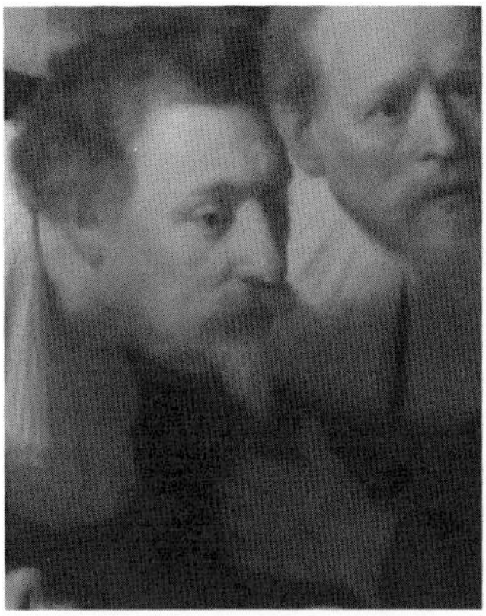

Soul mate: *someone for whom you have a deep affinity*

- Person, individual,. someone,. somebody., mortal,. soul > lover > soul mate

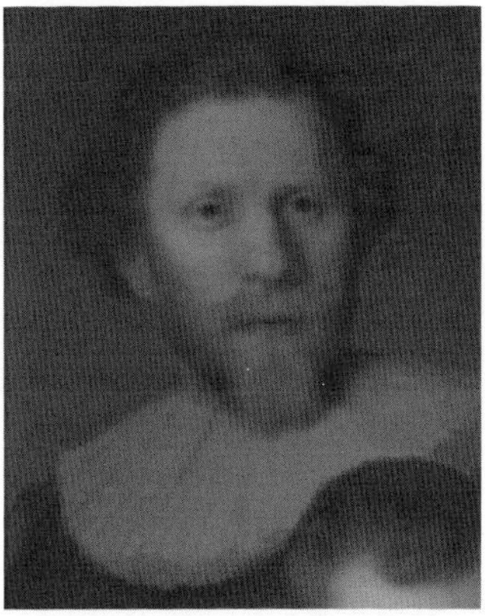

First offender: *someone convicted for the first time*

- Person, individual,. someone,. somebody., mortal,. soul > bad person > wrongdoer,. offender > convict > first offender

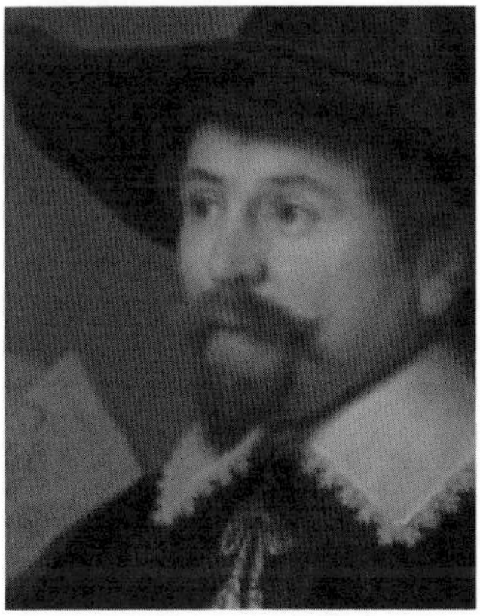

Cigar smoker: a smoker of cigars

- Person, individual,. someone,. somebody., mortal,. soul > user > consumer > smoker, tobacco user > cigar smoker

FIGURE 1.2

ImageNet Roulette detailed categorization based on image of Rembrandt van Rijn's *The Anatomy Lesson of Dr. Nicolaes Tulp* (1632). Image: Author, with permission of Trevor Paglen Studio.

In their article, Crawford and Paglen focus on the ways in which *people* are labeled. These tags are often racist, sexist, classist, homophobic, ableist, and in other ways derogatory. Crawford and Paglen show how training datasets and their labeling issues have created modern-day forms of social Darwinism, eugenics, phrenology, and craniology. In other words, image recognition software often reads moral qualities, personality, intelligence, criminality, and other assumptions into external appearances. Like the nineteenth-century statistical criminology of Francis Galton, who famously thought he could determine a criminal look on the basis of compositing photographs, few computer science researchers care to look under the hood of their datasets and investigate the biases and politics behind the categorization presented there. As Crawford and Paglen argue, "ImageNet is an object lesson, if you will, in what happens when people are categorized like objects."[16] Sometimes, however, even labeling objects like objects can be problematic. As evidenced by the training sets profiled below, the categorization of objects—artworks—can be just as political as the labels given to people.

Compared to Crawford and Paglen's work on ImageNet or to Exposing AI (formerly MegaPixels), another artistic research project that critiques facial recognition data collection, the use of art-historical images in computer vision research seems, on the surface, more innocuous.[17] However, as most art historians recognize, categorizing art can be similarly fraught. Svetlana Alpers writes, "Style, as engaged in the study of art, has always had a radically historical bias."[18] Alpers specifically cites how style is constantly measured by and revolves around comparisons to Italian Renaissance painting, but the radical historical bias of style can also be considered in a broader sense.

The university discipline of art history arose in the late nineteenth century in tandem with other scientific fields that tried to quantify culture. In doing so, they helped legitimize the view that Western art and culture were more developed and therefore superior to the art and culture of the rest of the world. With its early pseudoscientific taxonomic systems and supposedly objective or neutral parameters by which to measure art, Western art historians could justify dismissing the rest of the world as "primitive" and, by extension, justify the colonialization and subjugation of non-Western peoples. Western art was conceived as a progressive historical trajectory, whereas the art of other cultures was seen as ahistorical, remaining more or less stagnant through time. As much as the discipline of art history has made strides to abolish these original sins by altering or critiquing the traditional Western canon, the modernist ideas of progress underpinning it are embedded not only in the canon as a scholarly construct but also in art practice at various points in time. So, the canon and its biases remain difficult to shake.

For most of the research papers profiled in this analysis, art—in particular, Western art—is assumed to be universally relevant and exceptional. The biases and pseudoscientific taxonomies that contributed to what we now hold up as the canon of Western art are still very rarely acknowledged outside the fields of art and art history. The "genius" of Western art has become a global brand, and people from all over the world flock to see the works of artists like Leonardo da Vinci, Vincent van Gogh, and Pablo Picasso. The status of canonical works and the categories that art historians have previously assigned to them is unquestioned. As the creators of Painting-91 write, "Be it a Picasso, a Van Gogh or a Monet masterpiece, paintings are enjoyed by everyone."[19] Rarely are issues of power and representation addressed in the compilation of such databases. However, the way in which artworks are selected, categorized, exhibited, bought, and sold is an inherently political process. No matter what method of quantitative analysis is employed, the *selection* of images to investigate is almost always exclusively composed of canonical Western paintings.

One might then assume that just "looking" at the external appearance of artworks, rather than at how art historians have previously labeled them, would solve the problem of historical bias in art categorization—arranging things by line, shape, and color rather than qualitative labels. In the late 1990s, researchers were already concerned that text-based retrieval methods for art historical images, based on metadata, were inadequate.[20] They proposed that images instead be analyzed and subsequently retrieved or categorized on the basis of visual features (i.e., the formal qualities of the work analyzed through shape, line, color, contrast, composition, etc.). Colombo and colleagues list three reasons why they see textual annotation as insufficient:

1. It's too expensive to go through manual annotation with large databases.
2. Annotation is subjective (generally, the annotator and the user are different persons).
3. Keywords typically don't support retrieval by similarity.[21]

Mechanical Turk, voluntary wiki collaboration, and other outsourced/crowdsourcing schemes have, to a large extent, solved the first concern of Colombo and colleagues, despite how exploitative and biased they can be. Their second point, however, gets to the roots of why image database retrieval has turned to formalist analysis: its assumed superior objectivity compared to textual annotation. The third point demonstrates the extent to which computer image recognition is, to put it reductively, a large-scale matching game. The assumption is that the core aim in the study of art is to find groups of images that look similar. This erases the context of the artwork. Not only can this lead to pseudomorphism, which conflates works that have no historical relationship whatsoever with one another on the basis of ostensibly similar composition or appearance, but it disregards the importance of power relationships in the development of artworks at different points in history.

The research presented in this chapter takes the computer vision approach that Colombo and colleagues outline. If the primary goal for the research is to categorize artworks on the basis of style, researchers must use training sets with textual annotation before running untrained test images through the system and assigning them to preexisting categories. This is known as supervised learning. When image data is not sorted according to predetermined categories but instead grouped into clusters on the basis of patterns identified in the data, it is called unsupervised learning. These two types of machine learning have related but distinctive critical issues with respect to analyzing artworks. In the specific case of artwork categorization, the limit of supervised learning is that the labels given to the image data are assumed to be objective and discrete, and to correspond directly to the formal qualities of the artwork. The limit of unsupervised learning is that groupings are purely formal and that researchers must ascribe meaning to the generated clusters strictly on the basis of pattern recognition and similarity between image data.[22] Lev Manovich has positioned himself as a key advocate of the use of unsupervised machine learning techniques in the study of art history.[23]

I will return to this shortly, but first I will build an understanding, citing specific examples, of how computer vision researchers have approached categorization by style using machine learning models.

THE SEMANTIC GAP

In machine learning terms, style is considered a "high level semantic category."[24] This means that style is a label that is determined by a complex interplay of subjective reasoning and previous experience, which is typical of human intelligence but difficult for a machine. In describing the so-called semantic gap in image retrieval systems, Liu and colleagues write:

> The fundamental difference between content-based and text-based retrieval systems is that the human interaction is an indispensable part of the latter system. Humans tend to use high-level features (concepts), such as keywords, text descriptors, to interpret images and measure their similarity. While the features automatically extracted using computer vision techniques are mostly low-level features (color, texture, shape, spatial layout, etc.). In general, there is no direct link between the high-level concepts and the low-level features. Though many sophisticated algorithms have been designed to describe color, shape, and texture features, these algorithms cannot adequately model image semantics and have many limitations when dealing with broad content image databases.[25]

In other words, algorithms are adept at identifying the formal qualities of an image, but they find it difficult to determine the style of an unknown artwork even when they have been "shown" many examples of that style. Although scientists may try to interpret correlations between these low-level and high-level qualities, there is no intrinsic relationship between the two. Since Liu and colleagues published their paper in the mid-2000s, however, the rise of machine learning techniques has revolutionized the field. "Thinking and reasoning" algorithms that learn from past "experience" can now be used to try to close this semantic gap in image retrieval and are growing in sophistication.

Belgian artist René Magritte is repeatedly cited in discussions of machine learning and artwork recognition.[26] This is most likely owing to the semiotic nature of his work. Paintings like *The Treachery of Images* (1929), in which a painted representation of a pipe appears alongside the text "*Ceci n'est pas une pipe"* (This is not a pipe), demonstrate the extent to which style may not be correlated with image content. Zujovic and colleagues state, "The content, rather than the technique, makes this a canonical work of surrealism, although the technique is similar to that of Realism. Extracting semantic content from digital media is a separate task; this paper focuses on classification using technical features."[27] Magritte's work may not be as much an outlier as Zujovic and colleagues term it, however. His conceptually driven works are semiotic puzzles that meditate on the disconnect between image, word, and thought.[28] This is the domain in which machine learning researchers operate as well, navigating these disconnects as they try to bridge the semantic gap.

This means that the relationship between the words that we use to label objects and their representations is not as stable or concrete as machine learning research needs it to be to function properly. Crawford and Paglen write:

> Amid the heyday of phrenology and "criminal anthropology," the artist René Magritte completed a painting of a pipe and coupled it with the words "Ceci n'est pas une pipe." . . . The contrast between Magritte and the physiognomists' approach to representation speaks to two very different conceptions of the fundamental relationship between images and their labels, and of representation itself. For the physiognomists, there was an underlying faith that the relationship between an image of a person and the character of that person was inscribed in the images themselves. Magritte's assumption was almost diametrically opposed: that images in and of themselves have, at best, a very unstable relationship to the things seem to represent, one that can be sculpted by whoever has the power to say what a particular image means. For Magritte, the meaning of images is relational, open to contestation. At first blush, Magritte's painting might seem like a simple semiotic stunt, but the underlying dynamic Magritte underlines in the painting points to a much broader politics of representation and self-representation.[29]

Essentially, Magritte points to the gray areas that permeate taxonomic structures, including basic textual/linguistic labels that we give to objects and their representations. Whereas Zujovic and colleagues hold up *The Treachery of Images* as an outlier—an exception to the assumption that style is stable in relation to appearance—this instability permeates all images.

There is one further way in which machine learning research mirrors Magritte's work. Quantitative analysis, sorting, and labeling of artworks in computer vision and machine learning are done via digital reproductions of those artworks, which are often low resolution or in altered formats. Some researchers attempt to circumvent this loss of detail by using subregions of images rather than distorting whole images.[30] Nevertheless, the formal parameters that are used for these tasks are not quite the same as those that an art historian might use when faced with a comparison between two physical paintings and their materials: paint and support structure. Both the art historian looking at the paintings and the computer scientist looking at the digital reproductions might look at color as a basis for comparison, but the computer scientist investigates color in a quantitative sense—on the level of pixels, represented by histograms (figure 1.3). There is a fundamental paradigm shift that occurs when artworks are translated into digital form that cannot be wholly discounted. We might think the digital reproduction of Magritte's *Treachery of Images* on WikiArt *is* Magritte's *Treachery of Images*, but it in fact sits on unstable territory in this regard.

ARTIFICIAL ARTHISTORIAN

In order to better understand how art datasets are compiled and used in computer science research, I have analyzed a selection of the most often-cited and methodologically innovative publications on automated style classification of fine art images, covering a roughly fifteen-year period. A detailed table of these articles can be found in the appendix, which lists the selection of articles alongside a general description of the content of their datasets, the source of the images, and the style categories that they assess. In addition to style classification, most of this research also identifies additional parameters through visual analysis of images, such as artist. In what follows, however, I focus solely on the category of style. The first article listed in the table is from 2005 and therefore no longer cutting-edge computer vision research. I begin here, however, in order to look at the trajectory of development in art datasets and understand the goals of this type of research historically.

In this article, Günsel and colleagues outline an art classification and indexing system that they call ArtHistorian, which was designed to help

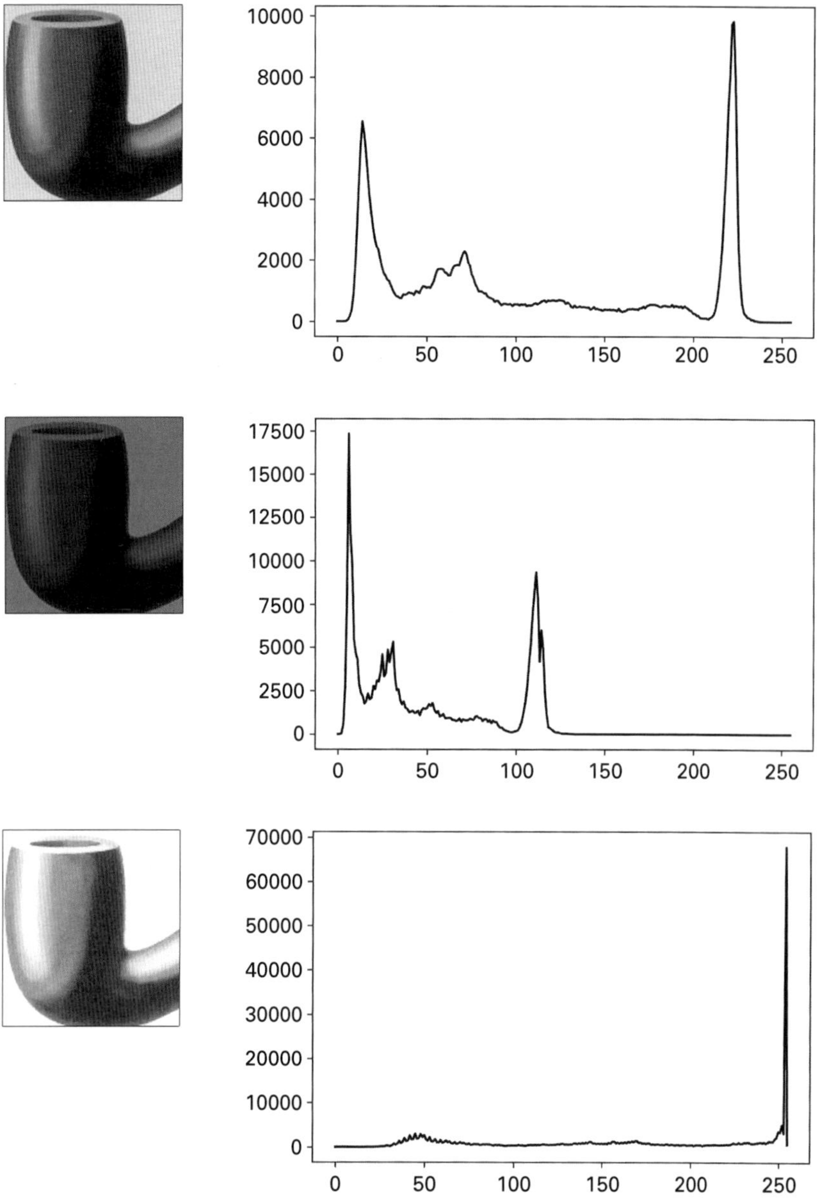

FIGURE 1.3
Grayscale histograms of three different image details with varying brightness. Image: Author.

database users retrieve art images by analyzing the contents of the image according to a set of features extracted from it.[31] By naming the system ArtHistorian, the researchers anthropomorphized it as an artificial expert of sorts. The user, on the other hand, was assumed to be far less intelligent or reflective. The authors of this paper make the somewhat mystifying statement that, "While designing an image indexing system, it is reasonable to expect that art paintings with similar visual content will be almost equally interesting to users."[32] Even so, Günsel and colleagues, like many of the researchers cited in this chapter, see the utility and application of their work in the context of art historical research and collections.[33]

Zujovic and colleagues point to the "clear utility" of automated sorting mechanisms for museums and websites to order large-scale digital image collections. They take this one step further, however, implying that they not only aim to aid in sorting existing art historical works but also in classifying previously unclassified contemporary work: "Digital captures of artistic paintings are pervasive on the Internet and in personal collections. These encompass the works of the Old Masters which have been scrutinized and classified by human experts, as well as the work of current painters whose work is appreciated but not classified."[34] It must be noted that this type of formalist classification of contemporary painting may well be meaningless, as it ignores the highly controlled gatekeeping mechanisms of the contemporary art world. Contemporary painting is often defined by the educational background of the artist, the way that artist is engaged in contemporary art discourse, and the artist's representation in certain biennials/exhibitions and by particular well-respected contemporary art galleries that participate in the global contemporary art market. Nevertheless, the implication is that, with the help of unsupervised machine learning, art historians will be able to create new categories for contemporary painting on the basis of objective assessment of the visual qualities. Looking at the contemporary art world, however, it is clear that art's importance is not based on objective visual qualities.

Strezoski and Worring similarly speculate on the utility of automated systems for categorizing the uncategorized. But, in their case, they see potential in these systems to predict *future* art trends/styles. They write, "Traveling in a future direction is also feasible, whereby knowing the past trends in the world's artistic scene, we can try to predict what art would look like 200 years from now or learn about different influences affecting its future."[35] This, of course, assumes that the way style is used and defined has been constant in the past and will continue consistently in the future. In essence, it assumes that style can be mathematically modeled in an accurate way. It also assumes that the concept of style is relevant for contemporary art. Media and materials have changed significantly over time, and hence future trends may not be predictable on the basis of a past sampling of digitized Western painting. Visual appearance of artworks is only a small part of how we now understand contemporary art practice. The global art world has expanded and diversified considerably over the past thirty years—there is no longer one dominant art center. Looking at the field, we see very little consensus on (or even interest in) categorizing contemporary art by style.

Despite these fantastical claims, computer science researchers are not wrong when they claim that, in order for massive art image collections to be useable for researchers and the general public alike, users need the help of automatic sorting and retrieval systems to find the images they seek. Siddiquie and colleagues summarize these objectives:

> Currently, paintings are being extensively digitized in order to preserve them and make them more widely accessible. Digital collections of paintings play an important role in preserving our cultural heritage. Automatic indexing and annotation of such painting collections according to style, artist or period would considerably reduce the manual effort required for such tasks. Supporting query and retrieval on such collections over the internet would make many rare paintings more widely accessible.[36]

Claims that such systems will help art historians in navigating masses of digitized image data are not unfounded.[37] As digital image collections grow, tools to sort through the mass of data will be more important than ever.

Problems arise, however, when computer scientists use terms like "style" to describe objective categorization of artworks and approach the task of categorization from a purely formal perspective. Doing so may actually be counterproductive to the work of art historians trying to sort through masses of image data. For example, one study on automatic style categorization seems to have analyzed images labeled with the style category "Conceptual Art" by using automated "brush stroke analysis."[38] Given that the vast majority of conceptual art is not painting (and therefore contains no brush strokes), this is a nonsensical procedure.

Style labels also may not be consistent with contemporary art historical scholarship, for example, or might not capture the nuance of the history of taxonomy. Svetlana Alpers writes, "One might prefer, as I have tried in my own writing and teaching, to avoid [style] terminology altogether: to insist, for example, on teaching Dutch art of the seventeenth century rather than northern baroque."[39] More pressing, however, is the risk that using historic style categorizations not only makes things harder to find but perpetuates biases and omissions via the reconstitution of a traditional Western-centric history of art. This is particularly problematic if computational systems are making decisions in lieu of art historians. Describing their aims, Saleh and Elgammal write, "We acquire these measurements to mimic the art historian's ability to categorize paintings based on their style, genre and the artist who made it."[40] Stated goals such as this are concerning. Assuming that replicating the art historian as a specific form of artificial intelligence is possible, this statement assumes that every art historian would have a single objective determination when it comes to categorizing artwork.

Art historians do not operate on the basis of static or universal criteria, and so an artificial art historian should not be expected to do so either. Some more recent research seems to go one step further than this, attempting to overcome the supposed inconsistency of individual art historians through automatic categorization. Mao and colleagues state:

> Hiring art experts to do analysis works (e.g., classification, annotation) is time consuming and expensive and the analytic results are not stable because the results highly depend on the experiences of art experts. . . . we present a unified framework, called DeepArt, to learn joint representations that can simultaneously capture contents and style of visual arts. This framework learns unique characteristics of visual arts directly from a large-scale visual arts dataset, it is more flexible and accurate than traditional handcraft approaches.[41]

This implies, of course, that a computational framework will be more reliable than individual human art historians. In fact, Mao and colleagues used an automated system to fill in any missing metadata information for the images in their dataset, which was in turn extracted from the information that could be scraped from an internet search.

What we acknowledge as art-historical consensus is, in point of fact, the collective effort of a multitude of art historians over the past 150 years or so. The introduction of computational processes merely multiplies this collaborative process. In her book *Artificial Unintelligence*, Meredith Broussard uses the example of AlphaGo, a system introduced in 2017 that successfully defeated the best Go players in the world.[42] The way this "artificial intelligence" operates, however, is by what may be termed brute force rather than original or spontaneous "thought" or strategy. The developers of AlphaGo used data from 30 million online games of Go played by real people to train the system. Essentially, this mass of games was crowdsourced from humans. When implemented, AlphaGo learns from these records of past games to find successful pathways played in previous games and determine what the best move is in a given scenario. Whether done digitally or analogically, the difference is merely scale. The knowledge is still collective. It follows, then, that claims of objectivity in image analysis are misplaced. There is a reason that groups of images are collected in museums and textbooks under the category "art." What has come to be defined as art has expanded and changed over time; it is not static or objective, to begin with. By definition, therefore, any dataset of art images will be biased for both what it includes and what it leaves out.

There are also clearly alternative uses for machine vision research conducted on art images that are not always explicitly stated. Khan and colleagues, for instance, hint at this: "An art image classification system will allow to automatically classify the genre, artist and other details of a new painting image which has many potential applications for tourism, crime investigations and museum industries."[43] It is unclear what exactly the authors mean by "crime investigations." This could refer to uses in art-related crimes. For example, AI systems are being developed to detect forgeries (addressed in greater detail in chapter 2). It could also mean, however, that systems trained to recognize faces in artworks might be helpful in increasing the robustness of law enforcement and government facial recognition software, with all the implications regarding privacy and civil liberties that it entails. For example, the authors of a study from 2019 created a dataset called MAFD-150 (Modern Art Face Detection), which takes on the task of identifying faces in artwork, even those that are highly abstracted.[44] Referencing the utility of such techniques for detecting art forgery, the authors state, "Deception and related forgeries can be accounted too using extensions to verification."[45] Although it is not explicitly stated, one could imagine that, if an algorithm is adept at finding the faces in a cubist painting, it might also be able to help detect the faces of people who are using face recognition evasion techniques such as "dazzle" makeup, camouflage face painting, and strategic face coverings.[46]

Another argument frequently made in digital humanities and cultural analytics circles is that quantitative methods allow researchers to study masses of material—big data—in ways that would be impossible for an individual scholar to do manually. In art history, this means making formal comparisons across a huge number of images—far more than would be possible for a single art historian without the aid of computational techniques. As the authors of one computer vision study, Li and Wang, write, "With advanced computing and image analysis techniques, it may be possible to use computers to study more paintings and in more details than a typical art historian could."[47] Likewise, Elgammal and colleagues write, "No human being would assemble the number of examples needed to prove the value of his methods for finding discriminative features."[48] Humanists and computer scientists alike make the argument that the scale of data is just too large for one scholar to comprehend and so computational methods are vital.[49]

Examples of humanities scholars who make this argument can be found primarily in text and literary studies. Masses of digitized text and the quantitative tools used to study them have been around longer than mass image databases and analysis tools, so scholars have had more time to use them and reflect on their use in text-based humanities fields. For instance, English literature scholar Ted Underwood contends,

> It is becoming clear that we have narrated literary history as a sequence of discrete movements and periods because chunks of that size are about as much of the past as a single person could remember and discuss at one time. Apparently, longer arcs of change have been hidden from us by their sheer scale.[50]

Most scholars still acknowledge the role of "close reading"—that is, traditional humanistic study—and advocate a mixture of humanistic and quantitative methodologies for contemporary humanities research. However, some take a more extreme point of view. Matthew L. Jockers writes,

"Close reading is not only impractical as a means of evidence gathering in the digital library, but big data render it totally inappropriate as a method of studying literary history."[51] What scholars like Jockers seem to forget, however, is that humanistic study is already a collective rather than an individual endeavor, even if single authors on journal articles and books suggest otherwise.

Nan Z. Da argues that, although one person could never read and compare thousands of books (or artworks) on their own, thousands of scholars working together within the discipline on a collection of objects *can* process thousands of images or texts.[52] This is what the fields of literature and art history have been doing throughout their existence: collating and sharing the collective readings/viewings of thousands of scholars. In fact, this method of working is no different from the way that researchers in the natural sciences operate. No individual science scholar can be responsible for understanding how a complex biological or chemical system works. Instead, an individual scientist needs to participate in collaborative research to help understand the bigger picture. Scientists are almost always part of research groups that work on a small piece of a larger puzzle and share their information with other research groups that work on similar or connected pieces of the puzzle.

A common misconception regarding humanities research is that it is scientifically faulty because it looks at a small "sample" of objects or works. In experimental sciences, small sample size is regarded as a sure way to produce misleading or flat-out wrong results. Sample size is still a relative quality, though. There is no objective size at which results become automatically more trustworthy. In fact, larger-sized samples lead to more generalization and therefore may obscure important or interesting outliers and difference within the sample.

In any case, humanities research does not generally make claims that a few objects are representative of the larger whole. Instead, humanists analyze works closely to understand their form, meaning, and context together with other works, building an argument that frames and helps explain a few specific objects and their place in art history and society. Lev Manovich writes, "we should be able to do better than simply consider a handful of artifacts and generalize from them."[53] However, art historians are, for the most part, no longer in the business of broad generalizations and grand narratives. The art historian as a generalist or an individual toiling on a particular problem alone is a straw man that advocates of quantitative methods use to argue against close reading.

Art historian Robert Jensen, for one, makes the argument for quantitative analysis on the basis of the supposed objectivity of a zoomed-out view of artistic canons. He writes:

> Art historians . . . generally share in the recent humanist distrust of scientific methods and of the positivism they typically express. They assume that in culture all hypotheses or general statements are so ruled by contingency as to be ultimately unverifiable. . . . Art historians, of course, must generalize; however, they rarely pursue those generalizations in a systematic and ultimately verifiable way. The modus operandi in recent years has been to apply a theory or theories to a particular object of study, without seeking to examine the validity of the theory. . . . It should be obvious, however, that individuals do not generate canons; whatever else they are, canons represent forms of consensus built up over time. In such cases, quantitative analysis is uniquely suited to understanding the collective perceptions of a discipline.[54]

Putting aside Jensen's evident disdain for "unverifiable" theoretical perspectives, he is not wrong in pointing out that canons are the work of collective endeavor. Whereas computational methods certainly make the task of managing and sorting large quantities of data much easier, they do not render the collective findings of more traditional humanistic methods "inappropriate," nor do they mean that a particular field by default gains a wider scope.

It is worth considering that maybe there is no way to completely zoom out and get an accurate picture of the whole. The top-down view has been one of the great modernist projects, charting and categorizing history in broad epochal strokes, but from the perspective of art history, global production of art is and always has been extraordinarily complex. Most of the artwork created over human history has been lost. No matter how much data around extant work is amassed, we will never have the full picture. Computational formalism has resurrected the dream of a fully zoomed-out view via the ideal dataset, a perfect and complete dataset of all human artifacts, but it may also end up being the methodological movement that finally forecloses the possibility of achieving an overarching view of the shape of form over time. Even if all the image data in all the museum collections in the world is included, which more recent research has attempted to compile, there is still an inherent bias. The data, not the methods, is the stumbling block.

Image Selection

In 2015, the Elgammal research group at Rutgers University used a preexisting art database with crowdsourced metadata, WikiArt, to automatically identify artist, style, and genre in images of artworks.[55] Using WikiArt was a game changer for the field. The dataset is much larger than those previously used in this type of machine vision experiment: 81,449 images from 1,119 artists. Previously datasets used far fewer images. For example, the aforementioned dataset Painting-91, which was published in 2014, utilized only 4,266 images from ninety-one artists and was compiled by the researchers themselves. Subsequent research has compiled datasets of hundreds of thousands and even millions of exemplars.[56]

Before the arrival of very large art datasets to computer vision and machine learning research in 2015, a common feature of this type of research is the vagueness with which image collection and selection is described. Often authors claim to have found the images "on the internet" or "World Wide Web," without any indication of which artists or time periods were selected and why.[57] Although there are a few studies that look at style in non-Western art, the vast majority of the literature attempts to extract the category of style from datasets of canonical Western painting.[58] In Saleh and Elgammal's initial study using WikiArt, *one* non-Western style—Japanese Ukiyo-e—is inexplicably included with a wide range of historical Western art categories. Ukiyo-e was also included in a previous study by Karayev and colleagues, which is noteworthy because it was the first categorization study of an art database using deep learning techniques. It seems that in both cases existing categories were taken from WikiArt without critical consideration as to their inclusion.[59] Additionally, one recent study included a custom Australian Aboriginal art category along with the typical WikiArt datasets in order to "empirically validate the efficacy of the proposed method."[60] Unsurprisingly, this study found that the non-Western styles—Aboriginal art and Ukiyo-e—were predicted with greater accuracy than other styles in the datasets that they used due to the differences in the formal properties of these two "style" categories.[61]

Given the lack of information provided by the authors regarding the choice of painters/styles, it is difficult to determine the exact reasons for their image selections. First and foremost, two-dimensional artwork (i.e., painting) was chosen as the object of experimentation. It should be noted that what qualifies as artwork for these experiments is exclusively traditional painting rather than images created using born-digital techniques. For the vast majority of the research I looked at, digital reproduction of the work is assumed to stand in completely for the work itself, even if image resolution is low and details of texture, color, or other elements of the physical artwork are lacking in the reproduction. As Saleh and Elgammal acknowledge, "Color and texture are highly prone to variations during the digitization of paintings; color is also affected by a painting's age."[62] Despite this, computer vision and machine learning research often tries to build robustness into their systems by using images of varying quality, size, cropping, resolution, and so on.

For computer scientists, consistency in dataset images is not always desirable even if it lowers the accuracy of the results. Using images from the same source may lead to results that are based on the qualities of the digital images themselves rather than the "content," that is, the artwork. Shamir and colleagues address this:

> An important feature of the dataset used in this study is that the images were obtained from various sources using simple internet search and were different in quality and size. While this policy of constructing the dataset can potentially reduce the classification accuracy, its main purpose was to minimize the source-dependency of the images and to verify that the images are analyzed based on their actual visual content, rather than the method of acquisition, quality, compression algorithms, or other artifacts that might be a feature of the acquisition and handling of the image by its providing source. Since the authors are not familiar with the exact details of the way the images were acquired and handled, no assumptions can be made regarding their consistency among different artists. For instance, if a certain electronic image gallery (e.g., WebMuseum) obtained Van Gogh images from one source, while Monet images were collected from another source, any attempt to classify this dataset might actually classify sources rather than painters,

> despite the fact that all images were made available for download from a single image gallery.[63]

This statement points to an important distinction between an artwork and its representation as a digital image: the digital image is not a neutral vessel but has qualities and parameters of its own that affect how it might be categorized algorithmically.

It might seem counterintuitive that the less one knows about the origins of the images in a dataset, the more trustworthy it is. However, it shows that computational formalism is actually in the business of analyzing digital images first and foremost, not the analog artworks.[64] The research profiled in this chapter does not address the material qualities of the work itself, but rather their appearance as digital content in an image. Digital photos have a totally separate set of qualities—a different "materiality"—from the physical artworks that they represent. They have pixel size, resolution, and other internal metadata that might provide information on the device used to capture the image, the geographical location where it was taken, and so on. In this sort of experiment, then, a painting is reduced to content. This is why Shamir and colleagues are worried about mistakenly classifying according to source rather than style: the digital images of one source might inherently have more in common with each other than their "content" (i.e., the painting) represented by them.

However, selecting a random and heterogeneous sampling of images does not necessarily solve the issue of categorization by *digital image* qualities rather than qualities of the physical painting itself. Like many other computer science studies profiled here, a 2010 study by Lev Manovich on 776 Van Gogh paintings used images collected by his students from "public websites."[65] The study sought to categorize the work by formal qualities identifiable through the digital reproductions—brightness and saturation—and map these qualities onto when and where the works were created.[66] A quick Google search of the images of one particular Van Gogh painting, *The Night Café* (1888) shows a variety of saturation, contrast, and other color variations in the sampling of reproductions available online. Which of these digital reproductions represents the brightness and saturation of the painting most accurately? How can levels of brightness and saturation be cross-referenced between digital images in the collections to create consistent measurement levels across the sample of images? Given the method of collection, these remain unresolvable flaws in the data. Although, broadly speaking, the deviations may not be enough to totally void the outcome of the data analysis, the study also cannot, in good faith, draw definitive conclusions regarding brightness and saturation of *paintings* based on these varied and inconsistent digital reproductions.

After computer science researchers have decided to focus on two-dimensional painting for their experiments, they often seem to select at random some of the most well-known artists and movements within the Western canon. As one paper puts it, "The artists we chose are titans known for masterpieces and opening new art movements and styles."[67] Because all the datasets in the research in the appendix include nonfigurative work—notably Abstract Expressionism—it seems that the researchers were aiming to incorporate both figurative and highly nonfigurative works in their collections to test the range and adaptability of the formalist analysis of each system. This makes sense, given the trajectory of the field of computational artwork classification. Some of the earliest research in this area aims to train systems that will differentiate between art images (i.e., paintings/drawings) and "real scenes" (i.e., photographs).[68]

Selection of images—including which preexisting databases and online sources to use—often means that researchers accept preexisting metadata for each artwork's style. Creating accurate (or at least widely agreed upon) metadata for an artwork requires a degree of expertise that the average crowdsourced worker on, for example, the Mechanical Turk or Clickworker platforms does not possess. It might be reasonably assumed that an apple will be labeled as such in a large training set like ImageNet if the task is presented to click workers, but it is less certain that accurate metadata for artworks can be successfully crowdsourced by nonexpert workers. Platforms such as Clickworker judge "correct" answers on the basis of majority response to a task. This model is based on the assumption that all tasks will be as clear-cut as "apple" and "non-apple." However, workers creating highly subjective image tags often feel compelled to guess what the majority might answer to avoid repercussions from their chosen platform for creating labels that the platform deems incorrect. One worker who labeled artworks for ArtEmis, a dataset of artworks tagged by emotions such as "fear," "disgust," "contentment," and "amusement," claimed that she was compelled to conform to what she thought the majority would respond and struggled with assigning a limited set of emotional labels to artworks from which she felt no actual emotional response.[69]

In the case of the WikiArt dataset, metadata is created via open volunteer editing and moderation. Their website states, "WikiArt filling system is based on wiki principle: free adding and editing the content by anyone who wants to participate. The quality and reliability of information is ensured by consistent moderation of all updates [*sic*]."[70] The Ukraine-based site does not publicize who manages the dataset overall, but the editing process is identical to other large wikis like Wikipedia. This means that, although much of the information on the site is detailed and seemingly accurate in the manner of Wikipedia, it is subject to inexpert mistakes and biases, and to nontransparent moderation. This does not always produce controversial results. However, it is worth looking a bit closer at one of WikiArt's style categories, Naïve Art (Primitivism), which was also used in Saleh and Elgammal's study as well as many subsequent studies (see the appendix). The juxtaposition of loaded terms in this category, listed under Modern Art in the database, deserves further discussion.

In Western art during the modern period, wave after wave of artists reacted against traditional Western academic styles of painting by turning elsewhere for inspiration. As more non-Western artworks were pillaged and brought into Europe due to colonialism, Western artists were increasingly intrigued by the different styles and forms they encountered. Professional artists also began looking to the untaught artists around them. What came to be referred to as "naïve" or "primitivist" art was, therefore, inspired by the artwork of non-Western peoples, children, and the mentally ill, all of whom were condescendingly considered less civilized yet purer in their expressive capabilities.[71] This fetishization of vulnerable and oppressed people was seen in the work of a diverse group of painters who tried to copy the forms of these "primitives" in the nineteenth and twentieth centuries. Artworks by artists like Pablo Picasso and Paul Gauguin have been described by art historians as "Primitivist" in style. This is a fraught term that is often used in a negative sense in contemporary art-historical writing, alongside acknowledgment that calling something "primitive" has a long, ugly history in racist and colonialist politics. If a style is described as "naïve," on the other hand, the term typically implies that the artists themselves were untaught and created work in an untaught style. Like "primitive," it has negative connotations and is also known (not unproblematically) as folk art or outsider art.

With this background information in mind as one views the works represented in the category Naïve Art (Primitivism), it is clear that the category indeed combines both self-taught artists and trained artists who mimicked self-taught and non-Western artists. The style category includes works by Paul Gauguin, Raoul Dufy, Marc Chagall, Natalia Goncharova, and Pablo Picasso. However, it also includes self-taught nineteenth-century American artists like Edward Hicks, Joshua Johnson, and George Bingham and self-taught French artist Henri Rousseau. For the group of trained artists, there are perhaps more general style categories in which they could be classified. For the self-taught artists, there are certainly more respectful terms that could be considered for their work. On another level, however, Naïve (Primitivism) should not be considered a cohesive style category, given that the best definition of these terms is "an artwork that is not in the style of traditional Western academic painting." With knowledge of this background, there is clearly an art-historiographic reason for such a label. However, it does not stand to reason why this would act as a single, stand-alone "style" category for computer vision and machine learning research. By definition, the category concerns context and not visual appearance. It demonstrates the extent to which there are overlapping style descriptors for artworks as well as how few works can be aggregated sensibly under one label.

Most existing style categories have a relationship not only to the formal characteristics of the work but also to the time and context in which it was created. For example, Cubism and Abstract Expressionism are tied to very specific historical periods and are not general terms for work that looks a certain way created at any point in time. By ignoring historical context, computer science research can unintentionally create incongruous datasets. Some of the datasets documented in the appendix contain overly broad or ambiguous style categories such as Abstract Art, which is ahistorical and sits alongside more period-specific abstract movements in art.[72] Another example is Siddiquie and colleagues, who chose to include "graffiti" as a style category alongside Cubism, Abstract Expressionism, Baroque, Impressionism, and so on.[73] Whereas some of the latter categories are far broader and more amorphous than others, they are all more or less tied to a historical period/context. The category of "graffiti," on the other hand, is more similar to "painting" or "sculpture" than it is to "Cubism" or "Impressionism," because it describes a medium/method of art production more than it describes a uniform visual style. Graffiti—if we define it as writing, drawing, or painting on walls or in public space—has existed throughout human history, even though it gained widespread acceptance as an artistic medium only since the 1980s. And given this definition, how is graffiti different from a mural or a fresco? The connotation of graffiti is certainly very different. In short, context matters. In addition to this, the graffiti sample the researchers use in the study has no named artists included, whereas the other work that they use does. The inclusion of graffiti might be useful in the context of recognizing and sorting disparate image content for the field of computer vision, but it serves only to confuse any art-historical application.

When computer vision researchers reference art-historical sources to any degree, they often present a version of art history that reduces artistic change over time to cognitive processes. Cognitive science research on art history tends to be Western-centric and to read scientific causality into the history of art, which is thereby positioned as a history of the progressive advancement in human perception and representation. Cognitive studies of art often assume that art history is an enterprise that continually grows more sophisticated and improves over time. An example of this can be found in the aforementioned study of facial recognition techniques applied to a modern art dataset.[74] In this article, Wechsler and Toor briefly summarize E. H. Gombrich's *Art and Illusion: A Study in the Psychology of Pictorial Representation* (1960) and *Art in Progress* (1976) by Suzi Gablik.[75] Although Gablik argues against Gombrich's particular formulation of art history, both authors share an inclination to make (pseudo)scientific assessments about the general nature of artmaking on the basis of the developments in perception and representation in Western art since antiquity.

Other papers listed in the appendix cite the work of cognitive scientists, such as neurologist V. S. Ramachandran. Although Ramachandran and his collaborator William Hirstein do not perpetuate some of the Western-centric bias of Gombrich and Gablik, they do develop a set of "laws" for art guided by cognitive principles. These laws are based on an evolutionary rationale of how visual information "titillate[s] the visual areas of the brain."[76] Ramachandran's work is cited by a number of articles, including Khan and colleagues and Shamir and colleagues.[77] According to Zujovic and colleagues, "Genres are a higher-level semantic category, and thus the digital descriptors should, in some way, have correlation with the visual features human brains extract."[78] Part of computational formalism, therefore, lies in the connection that researchers make between genre (or style) and the identification of visual features as a cognitive process. The assumption behind this is that a neurological (or artificial neurological) process can be identified that reliably determines and identifies the formal properties of an artwork. This, in turn, would lead to an objective/guaranteed identification of style or genre based on how the brain identifies shapes, color, and pattern.

IMAGE CATEGORIZATION

Aside from image selection and the inclusion of categories that are evidently based on artistic context rather than visual characteristics, there are deeper issues in image datasets with regard to categorization. These issues are two-tiered. The first tier represents basic art-historical errors or misunderstandings. The second tier is more complex and has to do with the way stylistic categories are understood as objective facts rather than imprecise, overlapping, and changeable terms.

As they pertain to the first tier, the papers listed in the appendix contain numerous inaccuracies in their style labels. In one way or another, many of them fail Art History 101. That is, if they were taking a slide identification exam, which is the classic entry-level undergraduate art history test that asks students to give the name, date, and style of an assortment of art historical images, they would have gotten some of the information wrong. Although many universities around the world still teach art history by employing this manner of memorization and slide identification, art historians have long recognized that stylistic categorization is merely an established guideline rather than objective fact. That being said, there are certain established style categories for different works that are more or less fixed in textbooks and art history courses.

Some of the first-tier type of classification errors are simple misunderstandings that seem to stem from a lack of art history education/

consultation among the researchers. For example, Shamir and colleagues focus on three modern art-historical moments: Abstract Expressionism, Impressionism, and Surrealism. They write, "Each artist was represented by different types of images (e.g., portraits, scenery, etc.), and no attempt to keep this set homogenous was made. An important exception of this policy is the early work of Kandinsky, which is substantially different from his signature abstract expressionistic style; therefore, his paintings from that era have been excluded from the dataset."[79]

Indeed, the three artists that Shamir and colleagues include as "Abstract Expressionism" are Mark Rothko, Jackson Pollock, and Wassily Kandinsky. Abstract Expressionism, of course, is a term that is now used exclusively for abstract painters in the United States in the 1940s and 1950s such as Pollock and Rothko.[80] Although the term "abstract Expressionist" *was* applied to Kandinsky's work by the first director of the Museum of Modern Art, Alfred H. Barr Jr., in the 1920s, the term is now associated exclusively with the aforementioned US movement.[81] So, this stylistic label must be considered wrong/misleading for Kandinsky, particularly when he is grouped with Rothko and Pollock.

This case reiterates Svetlana Alpers's critique of style. As noted, Alpers preferred to categorize the art she was teaching or researching by time and place (Dutch art in the seventeenth century) over style (northern baroque). Her reasons for doing so had to do with the way style is defined in relation to Italian art, but it can also be argued that style terms do not capture or specify different cultural milieus.[82] Although many styles are *assumed* to apply to a particular time and place, this need not be the case. Richard Neer writes, "saying something is baroque suggests nothing about its origins. . . . a fake Tiepolo is, potentially, just as baroque as a real one."[83] Nevertheless, stylistic terms like Abstract Expressionism have been established to such an extent within art history that limits on their definition in terms of time and place are implicit. Although Kandinsky's work is both abstract and expressionist and might share similarities with his successors in the 1940s and 1950s in America, his work does not grow out of the same context as Pollock's or Rothko's work. Where style categories are still used in contemporary scholarship, there is always a balance between visual appearance and time/place as ways of defining the style. This is why Abstract Expressionism has come to refer to a specific group of New York–based artists rather than all abstract and/or expressionist painting of the modern era.

Kandinsky proves a difficult inclusion for Khan and colleagues as well, who categorize his work as Constructivism while acknowledging that he worked in a variety of styles.[84] Like Shamir and colleagues, when Khan and colleagues find that an artist such as Kandinsky had produced work in vastly different styles, they typically treat this as an outlier condition because categorization (both human and computer) is easier for an artist who continually paints in exactly the same way over and over again. Lev Manovich, for example, makes a parenthetical aside in one of his papers, stating, "While Picasso worked in a number of dramatically different styles, this is not typical."[85] This is actually extremely typical. Most artists work in different styles over the course of their careers. The complete oeuvres of mega-famous artists like Picasso and, for example, Van Gogh are known and celebrated, but this is rare. In constructing the Western canon of art history, art historians have already excluded "juvenilia" or early work of lesser-celebrated artists. If an art history textbook includes one painting by Piet Mondrian, it will be one of his rectilinear red, yellow, and blue abstract works rather than his early figurative paintings. The canon typically includes one particular style for any given artist because it makes style categorization easier. So, Kandinsky's pure abstraction is emblematic, and his earlier figurative work is less known and therefore often excluded from a broad overview of Western art. This is an example of how, by using datasets of canonical artwork, computational formalism makes assumptions about the completeness or representative nature of the data. In fact, this data is often already sorted and ordered to make it as discrete as possible, per artist.

Another example of category confusion in Shamir and colleagues can be found in the three artists under the category of Impressionism: Claude Monet, Pierre-August Renoir, and Vincent van Gogh. Van Gogh is typically considered to be Post-Impressionist. He was a generation younger than Monet and Renoir, and he developed as an artist in a different country and context. The Impressionist circle can be delineated with somewhat greater ease than some other styles in that the artists associated with it socialized, worked, and exhibited together. Van Gogh was not part of that cohort.

Many artists are difficult to categorize holistically, as Khan and colleagues have noted. This brings us to the second, more complex, tier of art-historical misunderstanding: the assumption of objectivity with regard to style. For example, Khan and colleagues explain, "We have taken care not to categorize painters which clearly belong to more than one style and have only categorized painters for which the large majority of their paintings, considered in our dataset, were correctly described by the style label."[86] The assertion that "care" was taken in "correct" labeling proves this point. However, even the computer science papers that pass the first tier of art history—the slide identification exam—often make assumptions about the objectivity of style terminology.

Style has a complex history that evades scientists' attempts to concretize its importance or even offer a simple definition of it. For example, Mao and colleagues write, "The style concept is very abstract in visual arts, even those artworks that created by the same artist may have very different style, to explain it more concretely, style is something like *Brushwork* and *Strokes*, which is a characteristic way an artist creates the artwork [*sic*]."[87] Gultepe and colleagues also note the lack of "concrete" criteria for determining style. However, they write, "some visual cues from paintings may be utilized, such as color palette, composition, scene, lighting, contours, and brush strokes."[88] Strezoski and Worring, on the other hand, relate style directly to the concept of beauty, writing that what makes an artwork beautiful is style.[89] On the basis of their experiments categorizing a large art image database by style, they conclude, "In the eyes of an objective computer model with no appreciation for beauty, it seems that the styles defined for classical art are better suited to the artworks that represent them compared to the styles for contemporary art."[90] This is a revealing statement in that it claims that the model for categorizing artworks is objective and that because of this objectivity it cannot determine style (which is beauty) for contemporary art. The implication is that because classical art can be more readily assigned stylistic categories than contemporary art, style (beauty) is a better way of categorizing older artwork. This conflation of style and beauty is somewhat bewildering, particularly when juxtaposed with the "objectivity" of the computational system.

The history of style categorization is, in fact, totally different from the history of beauty in art. The former was part of early art history's mission to be a science of images—*Bildwissenschaft*, as it is still called in Germanic languages. It was a tool to describe artistic change over time. It was a way of ordering artistic forms in a scientific, objective manner (at least according to early art historians). For modern art historians, the concept of beauty has its roots in Kantian philosophy. Without entering into a lengthy discussion on the topic, beauty is, in many ways, the opposite of style. Following Kant, beauty is a subjective quality and results from a unique interplay between reason and sensibility. Cetinic and colleagues take the conflation of style and beauty a step further than Strezoski and Worring by attempting to quantify the relationship between style and metrics of aesthetics and sentiment. Although they acknowledge that the context of art matters, their stated goal is to connect machine learning techniques with "traditional formal analysis of art."[91]

Another example of second-tier misunderstanding is the work of Saleh and Elgammal on style classification. In the results of their research, they write at length about "confusions" between different categories of style in the analysis of their experimental results. Their use of style terms is not "wrong" in the sense of the first tier—they have evidently consulted art historians in some capacity. However, there is a distinct lack of understanding that style is not an objective fact and that its taxonomy is not a neat genealogy. According to Alpers,

> Categories are developed in the interest of externality and objectivity, freeing the observer from any responsibility for them. These presumably objective categories of large historical classification are then (silently) treated as aesthetic properties of each object. Style, designated by the art historian, is treated as if it were possessed by each object.[92]

This is an important facet of why the aforementioned undergraduate art history exams, in which students are asked to memorize and regurgitate period/style of an artwork when presented with an image, are being done away with in many art history programs. These exams teach students that style is a concrete facet of the work. In reality, style designations are messier than this.

Historically, there are often two or more different terms that artists or critics devise for overlapping styles when they arise. Sometimes there are distinctive "schools" of art in which the artists are grouped by virtue of the fact that they work, socialize, and/or exhibit together, such as the Fauves or the Impressionists. Sometimes there are *actual* schools—the French Academy of Art, notably—that determine a particular style in a period. Sometimes there are such loose collections of influence that groups of artists get lumped together despite their vast differences of style and intention, such as the Post-Impressionists. As Michael Shanks writes, "Stylistic attribution has little bearing on anything other than the discourse of style to which it belongs. . . . In this way style is largely detached from the social and political reality of people."[93] In other words, style is a self-referential category, not a constant and externally defined attribute of the work of art. As these examples show, even within the category of style itself, different definitions arise that might not be wholly compatible with one another.

This aspect of art history is often misunderstood by computer scientists working with art categorization. Having seen a particular work labeled in a certain way, there seems to be an assumption that this label is definitive and stable (i.e., that it is objective). Regarding the "confusions" that their categorization system produces, Saleh and Elgammal write:

> Further analysis of some confusions that are captured in this matrix result in interesting findings. In the rest of this paragraph we explain some of these cases. First, we found that there is a big confusion between "Abstract expressionism" (first row) and "Action paintings" (second column). Art historians verify the fact that this confusion is meaningful and somehow expected. "Action painting" is a type or subgenre of "Abstract expressionism" and are characterized by paintings created through a much more active process—drips, flung paint, stepping on the canvas.[94]

Saleh and Elgammal also note that there is confusion between Minimalism and Color Field, Expressionism and Fauvism, Cubism and Synthetic Cubism, and Impressionism and Post-Impressionism.[95] Unlike Saleh and Elgammal, Sandoval and colleagues recognize that there are historical reasons for certain "confusions" between categories, for example, between Impressionism and Post-Impressionism. However, rather than extrapolate from this that categorization by style is not a discrete and imminently solvable problem, Sandoval and colleagues write, "Future research directions will aim to reduce confusion between specific style categories."[96] Art historians have long recognized the fuzziness of stylistic categories. In the 1950s, Meyer Schapiro wrote, "the single name given to the style of a period rarely corresponds to a clear and universally accepted characterization of a type."[97] Despite taking pains to create an even more "accurate" group of datasets to test, on the basis of the work of art experts, the assumption of concreteness and objectivity remains in the task at hand.

The fact that the work of, for example, Jackson Pollock is categorized as both Abstract Expressionism and Action Painting for Saleh and Elgammal is indeed to be expected, but it is hardly an interesting finding for anyone with a passing understanding of that period of art history. More to the point, however, there is a concreteness to their description of terms that belies the more complex origins of these categories. The fact that Action Painting and Abstract Expressionism are "confused" with one another is not a result of their relatedness but, rather, their competitive synonymity. That is, they existed simultaneously until historical circumstances meant that one—Abstract Expressionism—ended up dominating.

The term "Action Painting" was coined in 1952 by art critic Harold Rosenberg and was, at the time, a way to describe the gestural, nonfigurative work of artists like Pollock.[98] As such, it is inaccurate to describe Action Painting as a subgenre of Abstract Expressionism, as if each term is neatly contained in a Linnaean taxonomy. According to Fred Orton, Rosenberg's use of the term "action" was rooted in Marxist and leftist revolutionary politics, and his fall from favor alongside his early conceptualization of this mid-century style stems from the need to erase both the critic's and the artists' communist politics in a staunchly anti-communist era.[99]

The term Abstract Expressionism, on the other hand, predates Rosenberg's terminology. He refers to it in the 1952 article in which he coins "Action Painting" alongside another competing term, "the Drip School."[100] In fact, the term had existed since the early twentieth century in relation to various expressionist movements in Europe and was, as noted above, applied to the work of Kandinsky at one point. The association of the term with abstract painting in the United States after World War II is typically attributed to an article by Robert Coates in 1946.[101] In his article, Rosenberg explicitly states why he proposes Action Painting over Abstract Expressionism:

> Call this painting "abstract" or "Expressionist" or "Abstract-Expressionist," what counts is its special motive for extinguishing the object, which is not the same as in other abstract or Expressionist phases of modern

> art. The new American painting is not "pure art," since the extrusion of the object was not for the sake of the aesthetic.[102]

Action Painting, therefore, has a much more complicated relationship with Abstract Expressionism, and neither of these terms can be concretely defined or put in a position of subordination to the other. They are politically, ideologically, and rhetorically separate ways of describing a period of painting in the United States. In some senses, Abstract Expressionism *is* broader than Action Painting, but this is by design. It is a way to position the work in a wider pantheon of art for art's sake and pure aesthetic expression, which Rosenberg rejects.

This discussion of Abstract Expressionism versus Action Painting might seem overly nitpicky. After all, the student taking that hypothetical undergraduate slide identification exam would probably get points for writing either term in response to a Jackson Pollock image without being asked to understand the nuance between the terms. However, the failure to recognize that stylistic terms are not stable or discrete can be observed over and over again in computational studies of this nature, and it is therefore worth pointing out where it occurs, even when it presents itself in subtle ways. For example, the creators of ArtHistorian, Günsel and colleagues, write, "The visual characteristics of paintings are determined by the painter and the specific art movement that these painting belong to."[103] On the surface, this is a true albeit reductive statement. Looking a bit more closely, however, we find that this sentence is written like an equation:

$$\text{Visual characteristics} = (\text{some \%, individual choice of the painter}) + (\text{some \%, art movement/art context})$$

This makes sense only if both the art context and the individual inclinations of the painter are static, discrete, and measurable quantities at any given time. In reality, of course, these are not simple, objective, or discrete entities that can be clearly divided up and quantified. Art historians, as mentioned, have long debated the role of social and biographical determinism in the appearance of style.[104] A statement as innocuous as this one, then, signals an assumption of objectivity in the identification of formal qualities of a work of art.

STYLISTIC DETERMINISM

If formalism can be defined as a methodology whereby insights and meaning are drawn from the external visual characteristics of a work of art, computational formalism similarly draws meaning from an automated analysis of the visual appearance of a digitized work of art. However, according to Crawford and Paglen, "Images do not describe themselves." By this they mean that the relationship between the visual appearance of a work of art and the way we assign meaning to that work of art via text or language is not a stable or objective operation. They go on to explain,

> This is a feature that artists have explored for centuries. . . . The circuit between image, label, and referent is flexible and can be reconstructed in any number of ways to do different kinds of work. What's more, those circuits can change over time as the cultural context of an image shifts, and can mean different things depending on who looks, and where they are located. Images are open to interpretation and reinterpretation.[105]

This is not to say that we cannot learn a lot about what a work of art means or how it can be interpreted on the basis of its visual characteristics. Clichés and truisms abound with regard to the relationship between text and image; for example, "art is in the eye of the beholder," and "a picture is worth a thousand words." Why should this change when an automated system analyzes a work of art?

Computational formalism often leads researchers to draw deterministic conclusions on the basis of formal properties. One example found in Zujovic and colleagues is the claim that "edges" are a good indication of genre (style). Edge definition is a metric that is used to classify images by determining whether borders between shapes within that image are strong or weak. So, a black square on a white background would show strong edge definition, whereas a gradient or fuzzy gray figure on a gray background would show weak edge definition. According to Zujovic and colleagues,

> In the first row is given a grayscale version of Jasper Johns's *Flag*, a good representative of pop art genre. We can see how the edge maps are almost the same for two extreme thresholds. In the second row we have Monet's *Sunset*, and the edge maps that differ a lot according to the threshold. Machine learning techniques should be able to capture this rule and utilize it for classification.[106]

In this example, we can see that Jasper Johns's *Flag* is deemed a good example of pop art on the basis of edge definition. Therefore, edge definition is positioned as a determining factor in characterizing works as pop art. This is a reductive and, one could easily imagine, misleading way to define pop art. Whereas style classification has certainly been driven by visual appearance in the past, there is an interplay between formal qualities and context that, although sometimes subtle, is typically present. Automation seems to erase all pretense of sensitivity to context in favor of a purely formally determined sense of what style is.

Early art historians—the foundational figures of the discipline—were taxonomists in a similar vein to computer vision researchers. However, although they sought objective ways of analyzing art and form, the role of time was always an essential part of their theories. Heinrich Wölfflin, for example, sought to understand the ways in which style transforms over history in a series of dialectic formal relationships: linear and painterly, plane and recession, closed and open form, multiplicity and unity, and clearness and unclearness. The idea of historical change in art was part of the modernist progressive narrative that gave the discipline its raison d'être. This construct would be heavily critiqued much later. However, if one compares the stylistic analysis of Wölfflin to contemporary computational formalist analysis of artistic style, treatment of time/context is the one conspicuous difference. As Wölfflin writes, "Different times give birth to different art. Epoch and race interact . . . to form an idea of what we must call 'period' style."[107] Style represented a complex interaction between time and an individual artist. Grouping together artists from disparate times and contexts or creating transhistorical style categories like "graffiti" is meaningless within even the most traditional methods of art history.

Elgammal and colleagues address this issue in a paper that aims to elucidate the relationship between computational style classification and change over time. They write, "classifying style by the machine is not what interests art historians. Instead, the important issues are what machine learning may tell us about how the characteristics of style are identified, and the patterns or sequence of style changes."[108] Elgammal and colleagues conduct their analysis through the lens of Wölfflin's methodology, which is an obvious choice given that Wölfflin was a proponent of methods that aimed to order art objectively and systematically. They argue that they have proven Wölfflin's model of art history quantitatively and that their analysis has created a "smooth chronology" on the basis of the factors proposed by Wölfflin. They argue, "The importance of these results is that they show that the selected art historian's theories about style change can be quantifiably verified using scientific methods. The results also show that style, which appears to be a subjective issue, can be computationally modeled with objective means."[109]

Elgammal and colleagues' research, however, does not "confirm" exactly what they claim to confirm. This particular piece of research has amended the Elgammal group's early style analysis using the WikiArt database and condensed some of the categories that they previously used to create a total of twenty.[110] For example, categories like Analytical Cubism and Synthetic Cubism have been combined into one Cubism category. They also acknowledge that style categories are not always discrete and that WikiArt's labels are not always "accurate."[111] The remaining categories mostly follow a trajectory of Western art from Early Renaissance through Impressionism to Abstract Expressionism and Pop Art. Ukiyo-e is still included as a major outlier in this otherwise Western-centric narrative. What Elgammal and colleagues fail to recognize in asserting that they have quantifiably proven Wölfflin's theories on the basis of the scientific method is that the WikiArt data that they have selected is already more or less Wölfflin's canon of art history. That is, it is already constructed around modernist theories of art history showing progressive stylistic change. Their dataset does not contain a wide range of art from around the world over the course of history; it contains exactly the art history that early art historians designed as an illustration of their theories around the evolution of style in Western art. Therefore, the experiment performed by Elgammal and colleagues is tautological. It takes a preconstructed formal trajectory through history and uses it to prove the same preconstructed formal trajectory through history by quantitative means.

Some of the more recent research in the area of computer vision and style does acknowledge the difficulty of using style as a category. Earlier articles show time and time again that style is a tricky and unreliable metric. The creators of the massive art dataset OmniArt, write, "One of the most notorious attributes when it comes to categorization is what makes an artwork beautiful—style itself." They conclude that their "simple model is better suited in distinguishing artistic styles from the previous centuries than more recent ones."[112] This is hardly surprising, given that the concept of style itself has fallen precipitously out of use in the art of the last fifty or so years.

Subsequent research still demonstrates assumption around the objectivity of style, however. In several recent examples, formal characteristics of an image are seen to directly relate to stylistic categorization. For example, in an article on a system called DeepArt, Mao and colleagues write, "High level visual characteristics are usually constructed by multiple low level visual characteristics."[113] There is thus an expectation that "low level" characteristics such as color and texture relate directly to "high level" semantic categories. In theory, formal characteristics define style. However, in practice, some style categories are catch-all terms for a certain context, such as the cases of Primitivism and Post-Impressionism. In computational formalism, any nuance regarding context is erased. Using the logic of computed form as a concrete definer of style, Čuljak and colleagues state, "Naïve art mostly depicts natural motifs so green color is prevalent, while realist artists have darker pictures that lean toward red tones. Cubists like intensive colors and have high maxima for each color component and saturation values are high [*sic*]."[114] This demonstrates how quantitative data can be used to make claims that, at best, are reductive and, at worst, constitute a misunderstanding of meaning in art historical study.

It is not quantification itself that creates misunderstandings between computer science and art history, but the way that quantified output is interpreted (or not interpreted). There is no harm in exploring a qualitative hunch quantitatively. In fact, this can be quite useful for art historiographic purposes. Sometimes there is simply too much data to count manually. For example, Robert Jensen conducted an art historiographic project in which he counted image reproductions in different editions of the undergraduate art history textbook *Art through the Ages* by Gardner, as well as other textbooks in German, Italian, French, and English, over a span of forty years.[115] His numerical output provides an index of canonical-ness that can be used to judge how canonical other textbooks are in relation to the main sample, and his explanations for patterns in art-historical and popular interest in certain artists produce insights that may not have been evident without quantitative analysis such as this.

However, Jensen's assertion that artists rather than art historians create the canon through innovation in form and style creates a situation whereby artists' exclusion from the canon is justified "because their specific innovations are so undefined."[116] Jensen argues that market forces and innovation in form drive and determine what work is important in the European canon in the nineteenth century. This is an explanation that the numbers do not objectively provide and, so, the quantitative method is merely an entry point for a qualitative interpretation based on historical evidence.

The great fallacy of quantitative research is usually not the method itself, but rather the belief in the purity of the data and its lack of bias. Counting a biased sample reproduces that bias. Data is produced by people, even when we cannot comprehend its scope without the aid of a computer. Jensen writes, "Individually, textbooks portray personal, corporate, and national biases, but when they are examined collectively these biases become less pronounced, above all by that which is held to be most canonical."[117] This is a typically narrow view on quantitative analysis and large data samples. Western art history, as a whole, contains biases, of course. Quantitative studies merely *count* (very quickly and very efficiently!) what we already have produced. The numbers do not tell us anything we do not already know collectively. The computer just counts in the way we tell it to. In the case of quantifying the European canon, it gives us a concrete tally of instances of certain works according to a number of different sources, but it says nothing about the broader meaning of these numbers. More instances does not necessarily equal more importance, more impact, and so on. Jensen writes that he wants to "compare the absolutely canonical with the merely important," and it is clear from his text that measuring "importance" is one of the aims.[118] Those of us who use quantitative methods, however, must keep in mind that assigning qualities such as importance to numerical output is a form of qualitative interpretation and not an innate characteristic of the numbers.

STYLE UNSUPERVISED

It is evident from the discussion above that supervised machine learning in the realm of style is a fraught enterprise. But what if we forgo preexisting labels on art images and just see how an unsupervised machine learning algorithm organizes image data on the basis of formal content? Ted Underwood writes, "As scholars have learned to compare thousands of volumes at a time, we have stumbled onto broad, century-spanning trends that are not described in textbooks and not explained by period concepts."[119] The idea, then, is that unsupervised learning might create a whole new way of looking at artworks in a more continuous way, rather than as discrete stylistic periods. Style, however, has long been acknowledged as nondiscrete by art historians such as Meyer Schapiro, who says, "Styles are not defined in a strictly logical way. . . . The characteristics of styles vary continuously and resist a systematic classification into perfectly distinct groups. . . . The single name given to the style of a period rarely corresponds to a clear and universally accepted characterization of a type."[120] The fear or assumption that style—without the aid of unsupervised learning—has unacknowledged gradation is therefore misplaced.

Nevertheless, in the interest of rethinking existing artistic categories, scholars have turned to unsupervised learning.[121] The excitement around unsupervised learning (as applied to style) has been greater in the digital humanities than in computer science. This may be because unsupervised learning analysis of artworks is difficult for computer scientists to justify. It requires a greater understanding of art history and the nondiscrete and nonobjective nature of style categories. There are, as a result, fewer computer science studies that use unsupervised techniques to explicitly determine style groupings. In other words, because style is assumed to be an objective and established category for artworks, there is no push to reinvent notions of it coming from computer scientists. This push is coming from humanists.

Additionally, the task of interpreting unsupervised clusters or groupings produced by such research would require an art expert to determine the logic or utility of the resulting clusters. Media scholar Lev Manovich has done a number of computational studies of images using unsupervised methods, and his end goal has always been to create visualizations showing the resulting clusters. Typically, these clusters are not explained in terms other than the purely formal elements of a digital image: color, texture, contrast, and so on.

Manovich asks if we can "think without categories," posing the question: "How do we instead learn to see cultures in more details, without immediately looking for, and noticing, only types, structures or patterns?"[122] It is an intriguing thought experiment. Categories are at the core of even the simplest human understanding. They are a key facet of language itself. Manovich writes, "Language divides the continuous world into larger discrete categories that make possible abstract reasoning, metaphors, and other unique capacities. It is not designed to exactly map the wealth of our sensory experience into another representational system."[123] The solution, according to Manovich, is to quantify the visual elements of digital images so that these can be sorted by machine. The distinction made is a fine-grained, multivariable categorization rather than more simple binaries. His speculation at the possibility of thinking without categories goes beyond the typical paradigms of unsupervised machine learning in that the endpoint of such experiments lies in creating new categories or patterns that are not predefined.

Manovich's methods, in other words, do not entirely eradicate categorical thinking. Instead, they delegate categorization to automated processes.[124] He writes that the first step is to create the largest, most comprehensive dataset possible—"ideally all artefacts." The next step is to "extract sufficiently large numbers of features."[125] These features are facets of the digital image that are quantifiable, such as color, saturation, contrast, and texture. They are the same parameters that computer vision researchers typically use. On top of these formal features, he adds "reception and use by audience" as well as "circulation." Because this proposal exists in the realm of imagination, we can take it as a given that these facets can be reliably captured. Once this all-encompassing data is collected, the final step is to explore that data through visualizations that map the images on the basis of various features. The goal, according to Manovich, is to "map and measure three fundamental characteristics[:] . . . *diversity*, *structure* (e.g., clusters networks and other types of relations), and *dynamic* (temporal changes)."[126] Whereas following this type of procedure may elicit some interesting results and, one can imagine, add some new insight to art-historical research, it might also create new categories that reflect, for example, the biases around what constitutes an "artefact."

Rather than predetermined categories, unsupervised methods create their "own" categories. However, as with supervised methods, the state of the input data is a limiting factor, as noted above for Elgammal's research seeking to confirm Wölfflin's theories of art history. The art image content that is typically at our disposal already contains the bias of Western art-historical narratives. Even if Manovich's all-encompassing dataset could be constructed and include contextual features such as reception and circulation, as he proposes, they would still somehow need to be conceived in a quantitative relationship to the formal qualities of digital images.

The importance that Manovich places on art's visual features has been previously critiqued by art historians.[127] He attempts to rebut or preempt such criticism, however, by arguing that "formalism" or "formalist" should not be seen as a negative quality, associated with the strictures of art critic Clement Greenberg.[128] In an essay on aesthetics, he cites the example of Russian artists after the October Revolution, who were ostracized and punished by Soviet authorities as "formalists." There is, however, quite a difference between describing artists as formalist versus describing scholars this way. Soviet authorities would have recognized that there is ideological content even in "pure" forms or they would not have tried to police the artists who created this type of work. Style—whether on the level of individual choice or societal trend—is the creation of artists. *Understanding* style is the work of scholars. In this case, "formalism" as an artistic style is not equivalent to formalist methods of analysis in humanities scholarship. The former is a characteristic of the artwork, and the latter is a lens imposed on the work as a means to understand it.

In order to understand exactly what kind of insights the type of research Manovich proposes would look like, he has helpfully conducted a number of data visualization projects over the years in collaboration with his students. These projects serve more to point out the aforementioned issues with his methods rather than to support its general uptake. We can disregard the fact that much of this research is limited in scope and methods, given the data and resources at his disposal.

One early project Manovich's team conducted in the realm of style was an analysis of a million manga images, analyzed as individual pages from Japanese graphic stories. The goal of the research was to understand which styles of illustration were "most typical" and which were unique, how illustration style had changed over time, and how artist practices differed.[129] Different manga series were explored and compared in mass using metrics like grayscale and brightness of the images. In one comparison, Manovich writes, "the fact that the brightness shifts very gradually and systematically over many months is a genuine discovery."[130] We are never offered any explanation or interpretation of why this is an interesting or relevant discovery with regard to the material under consideration. After all, manga images are not just images, they are part of *stories*. As such, they are not random or discrete patterns, and the narratives or context of the manga sampled by Manovich and his team are never mentioned in this analysis. How the visual appearance might relate to these stories is left unaddressed.

The conclusion of this research, it turns out, has more to do with the eradication of "style" itself than with any insights into why the visual style of certain manga changes in certain ways. According to Manovich,

> Manga's graphic language should be understood as a continuous variable. This, in turn, suggests that the very concept of *style* as it is normally used may become problematic when we consider very large cultural data sets. The concept assumes that we can partition a set of works into a small number of discrete categories.[131]

This is similar to the argument made by Ted Underwood above. From the point of view of quantifiable visual characteristics, style is a gradient. There is no Cubism and or Impressionism, but only a fluctuating set of visual characteristics with highly fuzzy boundaries. If these sets of characteristics and the attendant visualizations created by mapping them can be interpreted in a way that says something about the material being analyzed, there is no reason not to discard the old-style categories of the art-historical canon. The term "Cubism" might have pinpointed a group of artists in a particular place who painted using a similar visual style, but it was merely a jumping-off place to begin interpretative art-historical work. The decline of style as a key facet of art-historical research has, however, coincided with the decline in relevance of purely formalist analysis. Taxonomy together with pure visual comparison is not the primary aim in the vast majority of art-historical scholarship today (if it ever was). Computational formalism threatens to resurrect the problematic aspects of "categories," now with quantifications and terms such as brightness, grayscale, and texture.

STYLISTIC DEVICES

In this chapter, I have taken a closer look at some examples of quantitative analysis of artistic style from outside the field of art history. More often than not, quantitative methods themselves are not at issue in this type of research. It is a question, rather, of data and the assumptions of objectivity around that data. The focus on visual analysis of digital reproduction of artworks solves some of the bias issues with respect to metadata tagging of art images. However, the training sets are still often labeled by style, and researchers assume that such labels are concrete and objective.

Given that art image collections embody a certain narrative of art history, typically a traditional, Western-centric one, the application of supervised computational analysis methods to them produces insights that are already compromised by historical biases inherent in the data. Research that attempts to prove old art-historical theories, such as Wölfflin's, in quantitative ways must therefore be described as tautological in nature. They merely reproduce the conditions upon which the dataset was constructed—this time, numerically. Unsupervised methods, on the other hand, produce results seemingly untainted by preexisting categories. However, in their current form, they analyze only purely visual features of works and so largely strip works of their contextual meaning. This can easily lead to pseudomorphic comparisons among false friends. Within a narrower and more contextualized field, in which the dataset is thoroughly interrogated for inclusions/exclusions, some of these issues would be resolved. As it stands, however, researchers generally aim to develop a comprehensive view on art history rather than a specific one, and so they build larger and larger art historical datasets in an attempt to cover and quantify entire fields.

Although computer scientists are beginning to wake up to dataset and algorithmic bias, attempts to redress bias nevertheless often assume that there are static, permanent, "correct" categories that could be assigned to art images in perpetuity. For example, Surapaneni and colleagues explicitly acknowledge the presence of bias in their research using the Metropolitan Museum of Art's image database. It might not seem that important to mention, given the amount of critique currently circulating with regard to machine learning systems, but it is still rare for computer science papers to mention the possibility of bias or error in existing datasets. Despite this, the paper displays an optimism that biases can be corrected and "accurate" metadata can be created automatically, given the right tweaks to a machine learning system. The authors not only claim that machine learning can be used to accurately annotate images in the collection but also that they may be able to detect existing biases in the metadata.[132] This shows that ideas about objectivity in image categorization are very deeply rooted, and it is unclear whether critical questions about data objectivity will ever enter into computer science research.

In the next chapter, I move beyond the dataset to look more closely at methods and applications of machine learning, addressing these parameters from the perspective of individual style (categorization by artist) rather than general style. The category of artist, unlike style/period, can be constituted more concretely, using a mixture of material, computational, and traditional methods. However, the implications of this research in terms of forgery, fakes, and AI-generated artworks provide a new set of issues on top of the computational formalism profiled here.

2

Deep Connoisseurship

In the late nineteenth and early twentieth centuries, identification and classification of unknown artworks and artifacts was one of the core concerns for the new university discipline of art history. Before the nineteenth century, art objects were consigned primarily to private collections, which were inventoried with varying degrees of accuracy and detail. The eighteenth-century rage for collecting and categorizing antiquities was channeled into the nineteenth-century concept of the universal museum, in which artworks were systemically cataloged and displayed to the public for the first time. The modern discipline of art history grew out of this context.[1]

In art history scholarship today, subfields that deal with identification of artworks and objects, such as technical art history and art conservation, have increased their distance from mainstream art history scholarship because their methods increasingly draw from the physical sciences, such as chemistry, rather than traditional methods of authentication and analysis. The majority of contemporary art historians are trained to identify or classify artworks not as an end in itself but as a step toward interpretation and determining the meaning that motivates artworks' visual, physical, or material properties. For art historians who work in specialties in which art objects are not well documented, tasks such as identification, classification, and material analysis often form the basis of their interpretative work. Additionally, identification and classification are still a core component of the curriculum for many entry-level art history students. As noted in the previous chapter, however, there has been serious criticism of art history survey courses and their continued focus on identification of western, canonical artworks over the last twenty-five years. As a result, institutions have increasingly moved away from this model of teaching.[2] One would assume that this will, in turn, further minimize the emphasis on identification for future art historians. Besides these attitudinal changes ongoing within the discipline, technological changes may also further erode the focus on identification in art history.

This chapter explores the issues around art identification and authenticity systems that rely on deep learning techniques. The first half of the chapter will compare and discuss both traditional and machine learning methods for content identification and attribution based on artistic style. The second half of the chapter investigates how new deep learning methods combine with traditional authentication methods in the art market and how "creative AI," the field of algorithmically produced works, may affect notions of authenticity and authorship in the art world going forward.

Identification tasks belong to one of the oldest methods in the art history toolbox, connoisseurship. Connoisseurs practice a type of formalism that serves a singular purpose: identification/authentication of an artwork. Through close observation of stylistic details, they are able to identify and compare the unique features of a given artist's work and authenticate it.[3] One of the early proponents of such methods was Giovanni Morelli (1816–1891), who developed "scientific" techniques for identifying and attributing artworks in the 1850s. His method was geared toward the analysis and attribution of Italian Renaissance paintings, which in turn gave Morelli the authority to preserve and promote the cultural heritage of Italy.[4] His systematic approach to artwork identification was in part based on the claim that artists each had individual ways of representing incidental features like hands or ears. Comparing these features would, according to Morelli, reveal the identity of the artist.[5]

At the turn of the twentieth century, art historians such as Bernard Berenson in the United States and Roger Fry in the United Kingdom placed connoisseurial skills at the heart of their practice.[6] Today, the detective work of deciding who created a particular object, on the basis of stylistic details, is essential to the functioning of museums and the art market and often takes place in auction houses, commercial galleries, and museums. Moonlighting academics may be consulted in the authentication of artworks as well, given their particular expertise in an area, but authentication and identification of artworks is not the primary goal of art history scholarship these days. Meaning, aesthetics, and judgment all have stronger claims.

Indeed, detective work and medical diagnosis are perhaps the most accurate metaphors to use in characterizing what connoisseurship entails. As Michael Shanks argues with regard to Morelli's method,

> This involved no necessary concern with aesthetics, no need to judge artistic quality: it is a method with no necessary connection with art. Indeed, it has more to do with conceptions of disease and crime and semiotics, the science of signs . . . an artist is given away by details of eyes, ears and knees, just as a criminal might be spotted by a fingerprint.[7]

Richard Neer also connects connoisseurship to medicine, using the term etiology to liken it to diagnosis based on signs of disease.[8] It should come as no surprise, then, that Morelli studied medicine long before he developed his method of attribution on the basis of anatomical features.

As the previous chapter demonstrates, computational formalism has revived the category of style as a metric for sorting large digital art collections, despite the fraught history of the concept. My critique of computational categorization by style in chapter 1 revolves around the unremarked bias inherent in art historical image data. Computational connoisseurship—or more specifically deep connoisseurship, as I venture to call the applications of deep learning as applied to art authentication—takes the instrumentalization of style one step further into the realm of value. Svetlana Alpers writes, "Often the value of an object depends on assigning it a stylistic identity. This clearly involves treating style as an individual attribute. It is a major problem in classification that is essentially assigned to a group of specialists in the field known as connoisseurs."[9] Value can mean cultural value (i.e., a true Rembrandt painting will be more interesting to both academics and the public than a painting by one of his followers). However, cultural value is heavily entangled with monetary value in contemporary society.

The research profiled in chapter 1 was concerned mainly with organizing and searching large art image databases rather than authenticating artworks. A forgery would therefore probably not be detected by such systems. When artist identification and analysis of the material qualities of the work (brushstrokes, heat signatures, overpainting, etc.) are added to the mix, however, valuation and authenticity come into play. Suddenly, the academic exercise of sorting art images has very real earning potential. In this arena, computational methods are not only expeditious in purpose but also extremely valuable.

Morellian connoisseurship has more in common with computational formalism than its end goal, however. Both methods look to the granular and the incidental in applying attribution and categorizing artworks. In their research into how the Morellian method might be implemented computationally, Langmead and colleagues write that Morelli's detailed "schematizations facilitated attribution by staging comparisons, and this stepwise workflow in part helps explain why Morelli's method is almost irresistible to those interested in algorithmic logic."[10] Likewise, as detailed in the introduction to this book, Allison and colleagues describe how computational methods tend to analyze granular details, such as individual words or parts of an image, that might seem inconsequential to a human formalist. They found that their computational system for categorizing texts by genre based its categories on the occurrence of pronouns or narrative verbs rather than plot or overarching structure. Comparing this to connoisseurial authentication, they write: "Clearly, there is a problem with earlobes and fingernails: good as they might be at identifying the author of a painting, they are worthless at explaining its meaning. . . . There is something paradoxical in these traits that classify so well, and explain so little."[11] Given this, computational formalism may end up providing a level of authenticity detection that reaches beyond even Morelli's minutest details.

Computational formalism is at the heart of contemporary methodologies for visual and material analysis. Although technical art history has always revolved around the formal and material qualities of artworks, even before automated and machine learning techniques were developed, the use of machine learning in this area has shifted the focus away from the individual artwork to ever-growing accumulations of artworks. More than ever, authenticity relies on comparing an artwork to many other works of art. In other words, an artwork's authenticity is based on its sameness or conformity to a group of other works, analyzed at massive scale. Whereas comparison has always been used for authentication, the scale and distance from the artwork continues to grow.

The understanding of authenticity within computational formalism contrasts the Benjaminian understanding of artistic authenticity as emanating from the auratic singularity of the original.[12] Rather than lying in an artwork's one-of-a-kind qualities, the authenticity of any given artwork lies in harnessing the power of masses of digitized data—the more data points the better. Whereas connoisseurs and art historians traditionally performed an almost religious task of authenticating a work of art, communing with it via a mixture of instinct and acute observation (see figure 2.1), algorithmic authentication and fraud detection do not require proximity to the original. Only a digital facsimile is necessary.[13] Deep connoisseurship, therefore, discards the need for subjective knowledge that was the hallmark of traditional connoisseurship and, in its place, draws on a mathematical analysis of digitized features, triangulated into a unitary pattern pointing to—one hopes—the true origin of the artwork.

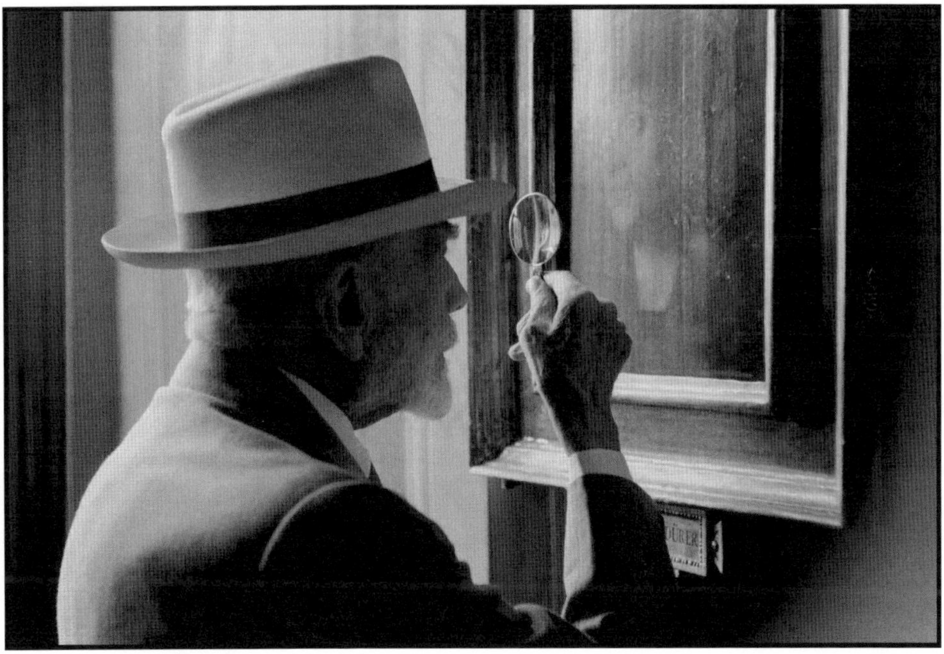

FIGURE 2.1
Bernard Berenson in Rome, 1955. Photo: Chim (David Seymour), TT Nyhetsbyrån.

CAT, DOG, OR VIRGIN MARY?

Using image-based computational techniques to answer humanistic questions in art history is, as I argue in chapter 1, a flawed endeavor. Interpretation, meaning, and judgment regarding relevance elude even the most sophisticated machine learning systems. However, there are many ways image pattern recognition and computer vision techniques can be used that have the potential to streamline art historical research.[14] Although younger generations of art historians may take for granted that we can access the majority of journal articles and an increasing number of academic books online, the ability to do library-based research quickly and efficiently has made the research process considerably less arduous. Likewise, image content recognition—the detection of objects, people, and places depicted—can be used to reduce the grunt work of art-historical research. This is one of the most developed and reliable areas of computer vision and machine learning research today.[15] Implementing this technology in archival research settings may help to quickly identify artworks in exhibition views as well as artists and other historical figures of note.

For example, a colleague recently presented me with a photograph from an exhibition of modernist Dutch paintings at the Israel Museum in 1965. She had identified most of the paintings in the photograph, but she was stumped by one at the right of the image in the foreground. Given my background in Dutch art, she asked if I knew what the painting was or who the artist might be. Unfortunately, the knowledge I had gained from past research did not match up with this particular time period. I had worked within a very narrow period of art in the Netherlands in the 1980s, but this painting had been created much earlier in the twentieth century. More to the point, however, my methods of research did not require me to cultivate an encyclopedic knowledge of all the art produced in the Netherlands during the period I wrote about. Instead, I focused on a few key artists in a milieu outside the mainstream gallery/museum circuit. Needless to say, I was not able to identify the painting.

This scenario provides a good example of how computational image sorting and identification might benefit art historians. Whereas scholars in the humanities are primarily interested in the historical context of an image rather than its "content,"[16] content detection can be useful in the practice of archival research, particularly with regard to reconstructing or understanding exhibitions for which there are installation photographs but no written record. Whereas art historians rarely search for, say, all the paintings in a database that contain birds, they may want to know which particular bird is depicted in a painting that they are studying in depth.

Within computer vision and machine learning research, there are many studies that analyze artworks specifically for their content.[17] This could be seen as a type of computer-enabled iconographic analysis. These systems, however, typically identify simple contents—a woman and a baby—versus a deeper iconographic interpretation—the Virgin and Child. Following Erwin Panofsky's formulation, this type of content—or "motif"—identification would be classified as pre-iconographical description.[18] However, as image recognition techniques become more sophisticated and metadata tagging more widespread, common motifs that have been replicated in standard configurations, such as the Virgin and Child, are increasingly easy to isolate and group within a given set of images.

While these identification tasks can be executed with a great amount of accuracy, we must remember that the only way that particular content can be identified in the first place is through training sets, which have their metadata origins in human-created labels.[19] Although the label of a simple object, such as a chair, may not be widely disputed, other labels are more fraught, as discussed in chapter 1. It is worth bearing in mind, therefore, that the computational system does not understand or actually identify either "baby" or "Virgin and Child," but rather a particular pattern in an image that has been labeled as such. This may seem obvious, but it is important to point out because it indicates the limits of computational analysis in performing interpretation and deciphering meaning. Nevertheless, image content recognition can significantly simplify art-historical research processes at the early stages.

Whereas there are many examples of content-based image recognition projects that illustrate this area of research, one example demonstrates the extent to which the goals or aims of existing technology is *applied* to art-historical images rather than developed from art-historical questions. In a project published in 2014, Elliot J. Crowley and Andrew Zisserman of the Visual Geometry Group at Oxford University set out to recognize whether art images contained cats or dogs.[20] The stated main goal of this research was to determine whether object recognition trained on photographic images can be applied to art images, which are considerably stylized. As a secondary goal, the authors state, "Apart from the challenge in its own right, this goal of automatically obtaining paintings with a particular object is of much interest to Art Historians who currently find paintings manually or from memory."[21] One can assume that the authors do not seriously expect art historians to be interested in whether cats or dogs appear in a corpus of images, but the implication is that art historians will find content searching particularly useful. Content or iconography identification is a narrow area of formalist study that, although certainly useful to art historians, is far from the first facet of ordering or identification that art historians might choose to isolate if machine learning systems were designed specifically for art-historical projects. In contrast to its diminished relevance for art historians today, content—that is, object detection—is arguably the most useful type of image analysis for commercial and governmental applications of machine learning technology, hence the outsized representation of research that focuses on identifying people, faces, and objects in images.

Given the importance of iconography to the field of art history in the early part of the twentieth century, some digital humanities researchers and computer scientists seem to assume that art-historical study is still concerned primarily with questions of identification. Whereas identification, as noted, continues to play a role in the institutional practice of art history or in preliminary research, it is not the end goal of most scholarship in the field today.[22] In pointing this out, however, I am not implying that automated identification techniques are useless for art historians. Quite the opposite, in fact. In the future, automating the task of identifying artworks or other objects—whether that means identifying their presence in archival photographs or identifying them on the basis of their materials, brushstrokes, and visual appearance—actually allows art historians to further specialize in answering and addressing humanistic questions rather than spending time memorizing formal features of artworks and methods of classification. The widespread application of such techniques may mean that art historians and art students alike will be relieved of the task of memorizing large quantities of canonical artworks in survey courses or in preparation for comprehensive exams.

The uptake and implementation of machine learning techniques in art history is not without caveats, however. In particular, it is worth calling attention to how, in developing digital tools, the ways that we can study a dataset of images are steered by the type of questions these tools are developed to answer. If the tools are developed to detect color variations of digital images, then color variation becomes a key area of study. If they are designed to find depictions of cats, dogs, or the Virgin Mary, then these iconographic studies of art once again take center stage in this "new" field of art-historical study. This is how computational formalism has become established in digital humanities research. Research such as this is not led by art-historical questions, but rather by questions that arise from technologies designed for surveillance applications. These biases do not preclude the use of these techniques in streamlining the research process, but they should nevertheless be acknowledged and their impact critically investigated.

In chapter 1, I primarily addressed how the assumption that style is a concrete category affects the outcome of computer vision and machine learning studies performed on art images. This was mostly a question of data creation and labeling. In discussing categorization of artists based on visual appearance, I delve into the different machine learning methods applied to this data. Whereas representation of certain canonical artists over others within datasets remains an issue, the techniques discussed below can be applied to any artist for whom a training dataset of their artworks has been compiled.

Value, Fame, and the Artist's Hand

Although chapter 1 focuses on the issues attendant to automatic categorization by movement or period style, many of the research papers cited and discussed have also developed techniques to categorize art images by artist. Often, the same (or similar) methods are used to identify the general style of a particular movement and the individual style of an artist. However, methods that aim to authenticate artists' works use different techniques to separate style from individual mark-marking as compared to the general style classification methods described in chapter 1.[23] Typically, machine learning attribution techniques using digital images as source material are trained to process and categorize brushstrokes. This means that direction and movement of brushstrokes or other types of marks are analyzed like handwriting to determine attribution, by comparing the marks from the work in question to as many established works by that artist as possible. As noted, researchers such as Langmead and colleagues have also tried to replicate Morelli's anatomical analysis in the digital realm with less convincing results.[24]

Whereas the category of period or movement style leaves too much room for interpretation and disagreement, which makes it a problematic means by which to categorize artworks, the artist/creator category appears somewhat more stable, given that it does not rely solely on style for its attribution. In other words, general style is flawed in its conception in a way that artist is not—at least in theory. Attribution of a particular artwork to an artist can often be reliably established, provided that there are multiple sources of documentation that support it.[25] However, attribution that is based on visual appearance alone can still be highly contentious. The more famous the artist, the higher the stakes. The infamous case of the *Salvator Mundi*, a Renaissance panel painting attributed to Leonardo da Vinci, is a well-publicized recent example of this.

Since its "rediscovery" by an art dealer in 2005, the attribution of the *Salvator Mundi* to Leonardo has been passionately debated. The attribution is based primarily on its physical appearance, thanks to the scarcity of definitive documentary evidence, which of course has serious implications for both its monetary and its art-historical value.[26] Although the work was auctioned in 2017 for nearly half a billion dollars to an anonymous buyer, it was a no-show at a planned exhibition at the Louvre the following year. This led to speculation that the buyers and exhibitors could no longer trust that the work was authentic.[27] Later it emerged that the Louvre had secured an agreement with the buyers in the Saudi government, likely Crown Prince Mohammed bin Salman himself, to show the painting, but that agreement had fallen apart due to a dispute over moving the Mona Lisa to hang next to the work. The Louvre also reportedly produced a positive authentication report to coincide with the exhibition, although a French documentary disputes the definitive nature of this report in attributing the work to Da Vinci.[28]

In a strange turn of events indicative of the contemporary art market, the painting was subsequently turned into a non-fungible token (NFT), a form of digital image with blockchain-encrypted provenance that took the art market by storm in 2021. This NFT was created as a political stunt by none other than Ben Lewis, art critic and author of the book *The Last Leonardo* (2019), which profiles the history of the painting.[29] This trajectory—from highly valued, possibly original Old Master to digital artifact in a trendy art auction bubble—perfectly encapsulates the way in which art market actors have increasingly thrown caution to the wind. In a rush to capitalize on the next big thing, they simultaneously chase record-setting rediscovered historical works of questionable origin and the latest in digital trends, which are guaranteed to fetch overinflated prices based purely on novelty. Before NFTs, AI-created artworks were the latest digital trend, fetching absurd prices at auction, as detailed later in this chapter.

Greed and the monetary value of artworks is only part of the equation, however. The importance of and historical background behind the development of methods for identifying artists through their individual styles is a tangle of academic, political, and market questions. As essential as value may be, one might question whether it is actually the style that is valuable—that is, the particular "innovations" an artist may develop in their work—or is it the fame of the artist themself, with style merely a means by which to attach a particular work to a particular name. Although a whole industry of art historians and laboratories exists to try to reliably determine the attribution and authenticity of a particular work of art, many researchers remain unconvinced that we can ever provide a definitive answer to the question of who created certain artworks, such as the *Salvator Mundi*.

Even digital humanists, who have generally remained more hopeful that new technology can help solve issues of attribution, are beginning to question the mathematical certainty with which some computer science researchers claim to answer questions of attribution and style. Langmead and colleagues denounce such efforts in no uncertain terms:

> What an act of hubris it would be to think that we could at any one point solve the problem of art attribution once and for all! Disagreement and a lack of complete consensus in an interpretive community is not a sign of its failure, or lack of "efficiency," they are signs of its correct functioning as this community goes about its work of continually producing meaningful, cogent knowledge.[30]

Such a statement demonstrates the extent to which the culture clash between the aims of science and of the humanities within the hybrid discipline of the digital humanities continues to evoke strong emotions. Academic questions about the ultimate unknowability of attribution questions are unlikely to satisfy an art market hungry for some sort of certainty to cling to, however.

To return to the metaphor of Morellian connoisseurship as detective work, the question remains: is the fingerprint a criminal leaves at the crime scene meaningful in itself, or is it only a means by which to identify the criminal? In the case of Morelli's ears and knees, the metaphor may hold true. However, for other markers of style, some combination of both artistic invention and artist's fame, complicated by history and tradition, must come into play. And what about value as regards artists who do not have what could be constituted as a "style" in the sense of pictorial style defined through the medium of painting? Definitions of style in art often, implicitly or explicitly, reference the artists of the Italian Renaissance, because they of course tend to most readily fit the definition of style that has been formed around their work.

Another important issue regarding artist classification is that the isolation of a particular artist responsible for a single work of art is often difficult—or even irrelevant—in contexts outside of modern Western art (from approximately 1400 to the present), in which works may have been created in collaboration or as part of a studio.[31] In those cases in which the value of an artwork within its original cultural context is not dependent on the individual creator, attribution of a work to a sole artist can be challenging if not impossible. In pursuing attributions for these artworks, one must therefore question the meaning of such an exercise, which may impose external values on the understanding and interpretation of the artwork. In the case of ancient and prehistoric artifacts, value may be entirely constructed by modern Western researchers and collectors, as the rarity of finding even everyday objects from the ancient world imbues them with meaning and value in the present day that they may not have had at the time of their creation.

Unlike archaeologists and anthropologists, who have a longstanding interest in the everyday and anonymous creations of ancient cultures, art historians studying work from more recent times have largely excluded anonymous or nonprofessional artists from their remit. Artifacts have historically been separated into "high" and "low" art, the former typically not considered worthy of art-historical study. This began to change in the 1960s and 1970s with the advent of the "new" art history, which alongside new media and modes of production *within* artistic practice began to look beyond the internal dialogue of the art world—successive stylistic movements and their formal analysis—for political and philosophical theories to understand the meaning of art. These included theoretical frameworks like psychoanalysis, semiotics, Marxism, feminism, racial and ethnic identity, and postcolonialism. Concurrently, new fields like "media studies" and "cultural studies" arose to address visual and material culture outside of the strictly defined Western artistic canon as well as new media and popular culture.[32] These examples of "low culture" that were continually dismissed by cultural critics in the early part of the twentieth century began to be taken up as objects of serious inquiry by academics and artists alike.[33] By the 1990s, those in favor of the movement to expand the field of research to include visual and cultural material not strictly defined as "art" took steps to integrate and reform art history's purview. This is known as "the visual culture turn" in art history and was hotly debated as a threat to the discipline in the mid-1990s.[34]

If we can assume that one of the primary aims of this visual culture turn in art history was to level the playing field and open up study not only to the "low" forms of Western culture but also to the visual and material works of cultures and groups of people outside of the Western canon of art history, then the moral grounding for such a shift becomes readily apparent. As it happened, visual and material culture studies were gradually folded into the discipline in the ensuing decades, leaving the fears and protestations against "the visual culture turn" largely consigned to the past.[35] Rather than replacing more traditionally minded studies of canonical works, visual and material culture studies generally coexist alongside them. I raise these issues at length, in light of the analysis in chapter 1 and the methodological discussion that follows, because the use of computational methods in the humanities has often been cited as a way to move beyond the canon and incorporate the broader view of culture, a rhetoric that echoes the imperative and implications of visual, material, and cultural studies decades after they were first debated.[36]

However, by replicating existing methods of stylistic and formal analysis, albeit on a large scale via automated means, computational studies are often nevertheless replicating universalizing tendencies that these breakaway disciplines were trying to dismantle within art history (and other fields). In other words, dispensing with the "big names" of art history may not be as radical an act as researchers think. Wölfflin's development of methods to produce an "art history without names" in fact served to strengthen rather than to minimize the universalizing tendencies in the field. Richard Neer writes:

> Although such histories do indeed dispense with individual artists, they replace them explicitly or implicitly with other analytic individuals. . . . The idea that one can escape from connoisseurship merely by omitting talk of individual artists is no more than quaint; it was, after all, Wölfflin who first advocated a "history of art without proper names," and he did not do so in the interests of a robust contextualism.[37]

Part and parcel of the turn toward the "new" art history was an interest in the causality of context over style.[38] Visual culture studies continued this trend through its application of theoretical over strictly formalist methods. In other words, method matters just as much as content in shifting how art historians think about art.

One cannot, therefore, operate under the illusion that identification and categorization of artworks based on artistic style may be conceived of—on a methodological level—in any other way than as inextricably linked to the value placed on the traditional canon of Western art. As such, nearly all the examples of artwork I cite in this chapter are canonical and Western, because such methodologies implicitly address this type of work. Although we may conceive of automating a technique to draw together the works of an artist or artists "without a proper name," the development of a method to do so is no different from the method that isolates Rembrandt's style. If computational methods are a manifestation of connoisseurship writ large, we cannot expect them to produce "robust contextualism."

With these caveats addressed, I hope to have cleared the way for a discussion of attribution using computational methods that does not operate under the pretense that such methods are a radical departure from existing methods in terms of their intention, though they certainly are a departure in terms of precise technique, scale, efficacy, and efficiency.

OPENING THE BLACK BOX

Technical authentication techniques that do not rely solely on a human observer, a connoisseur, can be divided roughly into computational and material methods. Computational methods may be used to analyze in-image features of digitized artworks, brushstroke patterns, or other information represented by digital reproductions of the artwork. Material methods, on the other hand, typically use analytical equipment to determine the chemical properties of the work: microscopy, mass spectrometry, X-ray, infrared reflectography, dendrochronology, multispectral imaging, and others.[39] This section focuses on computational methods, although the two categories of methods sometimes overlap when information collected by material methods forms the dataset that is analyzed using computational methods.

Deep learning is often described as an artificial brain, whose processes consist of what are called artificial neural networks. Although the comparison to the processing function of the biological (particularly, human) brain is more metaphor than technical reality, deep learning has offered interesting and unpredictable ways for machines to "see" and "think." What makes deep learning "deep" is the number of layers in the network. Layers, which are containers for input that transform that input and move it to the next layer, allow the system to automatically extract increasingly higher-level features. The main advantage of deep learning is that it automates the isolation of features so that researchers do not have to "handcraft" them (i.e., determine and implement them manually). In essence, the deep learning system decides how to handle the given data in order to meet the goals it is designed to accomplish. Deep learning is thus very good at analyzing unlabeled or unstructured data in an unsupervised way.

A knock-on effect of layering in deep learning is that this complexity makes it a black box for researchers, meaning that they can see the input that they insert and the results that come out, but they cannot pinpoint exactly how the neural network has arrived at the results given. This is because such models are nonlinear, meaning that there is no simple connection between weight in the model and the function that it approximates. Deep learning methods continue to get deeper, which only adds to their inscrutability. Buhrmester and colleagues describe contemporary deep learning systems as "hardly traceable" and write, "The explainability of a Machine Learning (ML) technique is decreasing with an increasing prediction accuracy, and the prediction accuracy is growing with more complex models like Deep Neural Networks (DNNs)."[40] In light of this situation, computer science researchers are working on ways to look inside the black box of machine learning and provide at least a glimpse of the network's "thought" process.[41]

One of the key questions for deep learning, therefore, is what happens when the algorithm is allowed to "choose" features itself? What logic or system underpins the freeform detection of features by a neural network? Some might argue that it does not matter how the system arrives at the answer, so long as it arrives at the correct answer. Whereas some "correct" answers might be checked by human experts in cases such as medical imaging, in which researchers might be able to manually check the accuracy of the system's predictions, reliance on such systems can easily produce biased conclusions that are not justifiable and not checkable. As posed by Elizabeth A. Holm, the dilemma is as follows:

> The goal of scientists and the responsibility of engineers is not just to predict what happens but to understand why it happens. Both an engineer and an AI system may learn to predict whether a bridge will collapse. But only the engineer can explain that decision in terms of physical models that can be communicated to and evaluated by others. Whose bridge would you rather cross?[42]

Even if we are given assurances that the system is 100% reliable, we may find ourselves craving a deeper justification.

In the realm of image recognition and analysis, researchers have developed different techniques that attempt to extract, freeze, or isolate elements of the network's "thought process." Feature visualizations are essentially images frozen in time that reveal or display something about the details the system has focused on in the process of completing the task at hand.[43] The level of detail that a deep learning system focuses on, which may seem irrelevant or even absurd to human readers or viewers, can be illustrated by these feature visualizations, which disentangle and interpret the processes within the black box.[44] Visualizations can also show researchers the differences between the lower-level layers and high-level layers in a deep learning system.

Computer scientists have found that feature visualization helps them understand, for instance, how deep transfer learning works, and art images are among the types of image data used.[45] Deep transfer learning means that a model trained on one set of data is applied to another set of data in order to optimize analysis. In the case of image analysis and feature visualization, a model such as Google's Inception (versions 1–3), which is pretrained on the ImageNet database, is used to analyze collections of artworks. In other words, a model trained on photographic images is commonly used on images of artworks, which raises the question of how learning from photographic images might be transferred to analysis of art images.

In their research, Gonthier and colleagues have addressed precisely this question. Figure 2.2 shows two feature visualizations that they have produced, which correspond to different higher-level channels and the top one hundred images from the target dataset that trigger each channel the most. The first visualization triggers a set of images that consists mostly of Japanese Ukiyo-e prints mixed with some Renaissance paintings, and the second set of triggered images consists of all Renaissance images. Gonthier and colleagues note that visualizations of higher-level layers seem more difficult to interpret than the lower-layer visualizations, which show clearer imagery for specific objects such as drapery, mountain tops, or the facades of buildings.[46] Visualizations of higher-level layers, on the other hand, seem to gather images that share a more difficult-to-describe visual style rather than the presence of certain objects.

In this example, the texture of each visualization is evocative of the textures found in each group of images. For instance, the manner in which gradients are used in Ukiyo-e is evident in the visualization. There are also some clues to composition found within the feature visualizations. In the case of the feature visualization corresponding to the Japanese prints, one can see sweeping diagonal compositional features, which are also found in the image group represented. For the second feature visualization, more dome-like features and rectilinear shapes and compositions emerge. As Geirhos and colleagues found in their research, convolutional neural networks (CNNs) tend to favor textures over shape in image analysis, which contrasts with how human vision functions.[47]

The utility of feature visualizations has not escaped the notice of digital humanities researchers. Combining technical and art-historical

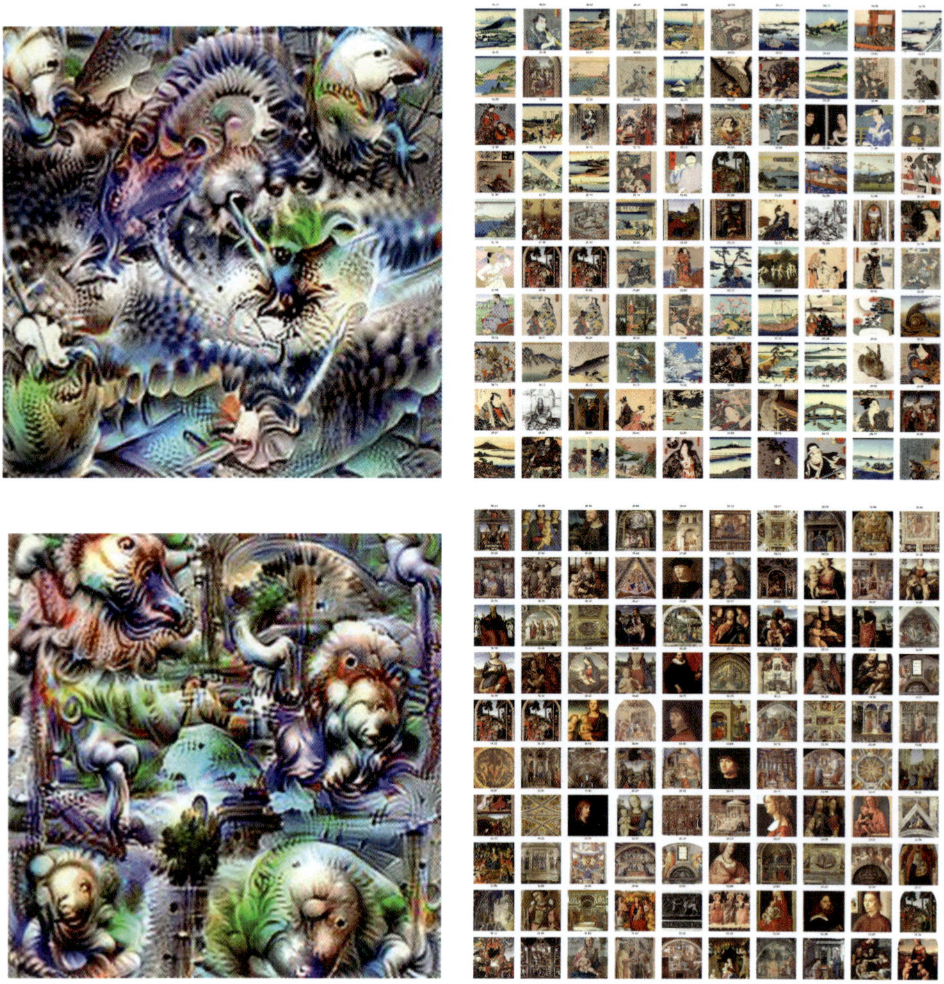

FIGURE 2.2
Two feature visualizations corresponding to higher-level channels and the top one hundred images from the dataset of artworks that trigger each channel the most. Image: Nicolas Gonthier.

knowledge, Fabian Offert and Peter Bell examine the implications of applying feature visualizations to art-historical image datasets.[48] They argue that, by examining feature visualizations, we may be able to pinpoint or elucidate the "perceptual bias" of the machinic eye.

Offert previously explored the ways in which feature visualizations can be used to "see" or pinpoint what the computational system "sees" in its analysis of, for example, artistic genre. He writes, "In assessing a dataset with the help of machine learning, the digital art historian would not only take the model's results into account but also include a large set of feature visualization images in the analysis."[49] In the examples Offert provides, created from an analysis of images categorized as either portrait or landscape from a subset of the Web Gallery of Art dataset, the feature visualization for the category of portraiture shows rough outlines of figures seemingly swathed in drapery. The landscape visualization is even more abstract. Knowing that it is a representation of the landscape category, one can make out rough tracing of a horizontal ground line. In essence, such visualizations show the ways in which the neural network *defines* a particular genre and categorizes unfamiliar images within it. Whereas art historians may be happy to accept that the genre of landscape is broadly defined by the horizontal ground line, they may be less ready to concede that portraiture is defined almost exclusively by the presence of drapery.[50] Offert writes, "Both results point to subtle (likely historical and/or geographical) bias in the dataset that deserves further analysis."[51] The suggestion of this paper is that feature visualization counteracts the "inscrutability" of the machine learning system.

Whereas the creation of feature visualizations such as these help pinpoint certain bias in the system and even the system's peculiar "ways of seeing," it is unclear how feature visualizations actually support the use of machine learning systems for analysis of artworks.[52] The issues of formalist bias remain—and, indeed, they are exposed to an even greater extent in such images. We see clearly the perceptual bias of the system toward picking out and perhaps exaggerating the importance of incidental elements of a work of art, such as drapery, which is indicative of a very specific (and unacknowledged) art-making context. In effect, what these visualizations show is that, although the category is labeled portraiture, the system has no understanding of what essentially defines a portrait.

Despite the "neural network" moniker and its biological connotations, the system has not "understood" exactly what portraiture is. Indeed, the insistence on equating computational neural networks with the workings of the human brain and "intelligence" plays into a long history of scientific racism, colonial dominance, and political applications of the concept of intelligence to justify existing social hierarchies.[53] Nevertheless, the system—within the limited parameters of the experiment—has successfully categorized un-sorted images as portraiture, even if it does so in a different way than humans would.

As Offert and Bell argue in their paper on the perceptual bias of deep learning systems,

> Objects, for us, are necessarily spatially cohesive. If they are represented by CNNs, however, they lose this spatial coherence, different aspects of an object are attached to different neurons, which, in turn, get re-used in the detection of other objects. This missing coherence does not interfere with the CNN's ability to detect or classify spatially coherent objects in images but enables it.[54]

In other words, the way that CNNs operate means that rather than analyze images as a whole, they isolate and essentially scramble elements of the image. The CNN "perceives" images in pieces and attaches those pieces as weights to a "neuron." As Offert and Bell explain, this provides results that we can more or less "verify" are accurate on the basis of the results of the process, but the machine learning system—we see on closer inspection—arrives at these conclusions in ways that are wholly foreign to typical human perceptual processes.

These differences between how humans and deep learning systems "see" need not be considered a disadvantage or a reason to avoid automated systems, however. Holm writes, in a defense of using black box deep learning systems, that we may in fact be able to learn from this other way of "seeing," which might provide new insights into the material at hand. She writes, "Although AI thought processes can be limited, biased, or outright wrong, they are also different from human thought processes in ways that can reveal new connections and approaches."[55] Holm provides an example from diabetes research, in which images of the retina of the eye are used to diagnose a particular complication from the disease. Not only was the deep learning system able to diagnose the images better than ophthalmologists, but it picked up certain characteristics that accurately allowed it to predict the sex of the patient. Previous research had not noted that there were such differences in the retina based on sex. One can see how such systems, coupled with tools that researchers are developing to open the black box of deep learning, might provide insights into artworks that researchers had not previously noticed and open up new areas of inquiry.

As is the case in other fields, implementation of deep learning techniques is not merely an academic question for art history. Increasingly, deep learning is taking its place among other traditional and scientific methods in the business of art, particularly in artist authentication services.

THE BUSINESS OF AUTHENTICITY

As artworks continually break record sales figures at auction, developing new tools for authentication is a potentially lucrative endeavor for researchers who position themselves in between the academic world and tech start-ups. Alongside existing material analysis techniques for detecting forgeries, researchers and start-ups are beginning to offer detection methods based on deep learning, using neural networks to determine whether artworks have been created by the same artist. Some of these methods function in similar ways to the analyses of style described in chapter 1. Most of the researchers working in this area are careful to state that they see machine learning authentication as a complement to existing methods rather than a replacement.[56]

Attribution of a work to a particular artist rarely depends solely on the visual or material qualities of the work; provenance and other forms of documentation—art's paper trail—are essential components of attribution as well. Fraud and forgery can occur at any step of the process, and often the most successful forgeries include not only the production of an artwork using period-specific materials and techniques but also forged documentary support for whatever story is invented to accompany the work. If the attribution of an artwork were merely an academic question rather than one of monetary value, the human experts practicing some version of Morelli's connoisseurial science may have remained the authoritative voices in determining attribution. However, given the vast sums of money at stake in the art market today—alongside a spate of high-profile forgery cases in recent years—there is a great deal of urgency and potential monetary rewards for those developing new authentication tools.[57]

The art market is unique in that it is almost completely unregulated and therefore ripe for fraud, forgery, and manipulation.[58] Entities that hold an interest in the value of art include artists (if they are alive), galleries, museums, collectors, and auction houses. However, a secondary economy of experts and evaluators who work with art institutions to analyze the authenticity of artworks also has an interest in providing attributions that make their customers happy. This economy includes not only traditional connoisseurs and art historians but also small scientific labs. According to Erhard Jägers, who runs an authentication lab in Germany that has tested Russian avant-garde works and found many to be fake, "Using scientific methods, we can find out if something is a forgery . . . we cannot confirm that it is genuine. If the examination does not contradict the attribution of the work to a certain artist or period, the expertise of an art historian is necessary."[59] Once a small market clique dependent on trust and personal relationships, the exponential growth of the art market in the last twenty to thirty years has meant that more and more high-profile forgery operations have attempted to take advantage of the high prices garnered for all periods of art production.[60] Time and time again, when authentication is left to human experts, a complex interplay of emotions and special interests enters the equation.

One example of this is the trial of gallerist Ann Freedman of Knoedler Gallery in New York, who was accused of knowingly defrauding collectors over a thirty-year period by selling fake Abstract Expressionist artworks. Freedman maintains her innocence, claiming that she too was a victim of the fraud, although there is certainly evidence that points to her complicity.[61] Interviews with Freedman in a documentary on the case, *Made You Look: A True Story about Fake Art* (2020), suggest that she wanted so badly to believe that the works were real—either out of greed or excitement—that she ignored any warning signs and red flags regarding their provenance and origin. With large sums of money on the line, dealers often turn a blind eye to obvious faults in the artworks they receive, a situation that scammers are quick to take advantage of.[62] Apart from the credulity of dealers, the Knoedler documentary also highlights how "independent" experts authenticating the works were motivated to claim that they were genuine in order to maintain their relationships with the gallery. During another court case involving forgeries among Russian avant-garde works, the judge quickly grew exasperated with the contradictory expert witnesses testifying, saying: "Ask 10 different art historians the same question and you get 10 different answers. Behind the experts there are diverse vested interests influencing how these paintings are evaluated."[63] The trust in human experts has been significantly eroded in recent years as cases like this are exposed.

The impact of the art authenticator's emotional investment in the work—or the will to believe that the work is real—is not a new phenomenon. The famous case of forger Han van Meegeren in the 1930s in the Netherlands, who fooled Vermeer expert Abraham Bredius among others into believing his forgeries were long-lost Vermeers, provides another example of credulous experts embracing less than credible work. As Anthony M. Amore describes it, "The opportunity to be part of the important new find seems to have clouded their judgment, a pattern that has been repeated several times throughout history."[64] Bredius even wrote a glowing article in the *Burlington Magazine* in 1937, proclaiming, "It is a wonderful moment in the life of a lover of art when he finds himself suddenly confronted with a hitherto unknown painting by a great master, untouched, on the original canvas, and without any restoration, just as it left the painter's studio! And what a picture! . . . we have here a—I am inclined to say—*the* masterpiece of Johannes Vermeer of Delft."[65] In his book on the *Salvator Mundi*, Ben Lewis similarly implies that art historian Martin Kemp has been lured into too-hasty authentications of "new" works by Leonardo da Vinci, despite Kemp's own warnings about compromised and biased connoisseurship.[66] Needless to say, the art historians and connoisseurs tasked with authenticating works of art have long been influenced—whether consciously or not—by their emotional and financial investment in the works, which has in turn allowed fakes to proliferate in the art market over the years.

In addition to human experts, authentication services typically include chemical and material analysis as well. Neither of these methods, taken alone, is sufficient to act as a deciding factor in authentication, however. Jehane Ragai writes:

> In spite of the crucial role played by science in identifying forgeries, one must be wary of blindly relying upon the results of technical analysis alone. Indeed scientific tests should not, in isolation, be the sole determinant of fraud, nor can connoisseurship play the definitive role in the evaluation of works of art. Intuition and a deep understanding of the artwork, together with a close analysis of technique, appearance and design, are essential in complementing objectively collected scientific data.[67]

Meticulous forgers are well aware of the various material analysis techniques used to authenticate artworks and so often scour flea markets and secondhand shops for era-appropriate materials, do research into historic paint-mixing techniques, or find other methods to give their materials chemical properties to demonstrate aging. Given that trust in experts has been shaken and that chemical analytical methods are limited to the detection of anachronisms in the materials themselves (regardless of whether those old materials were repurposed for forgery or not), the art market has sought new methods of authentication to assure collectors that they are not throwing their money away on forgeries.

The first deep learning start-ups on the scene are hoping to fill the need for security and confidence in an art market awash with forgery scandals. One art authentication start-up that uses deep learning techniques is Art Recognition, based in Zurich, Switzerland, and founded in January 2019.[68] The founders and managers of the company are Carina Popovici, a PhD in particle physics and former quantitative risk specialist in Swiss banking, and Christiane Hoppe-Oehl, who holds a degree in applied mathematics and has also worked in the banking industry.[69] Although they have no previous experience in the art market, they worked on AI applications in other sectors for many years and were turned on to the field of art authentication via conversations with an art historian. The code for their system, which uses a deep convolutional neural network, was developed entirely by Popovici, but the company has subsequently been able to hire a small team to support their technical development. Art Recognition is still a relatively new venture, without the accompanying academic research profile of some potential competitors. However, their board of advisors, who are affiliated on a pro bono basis, includes Eric Postma, a data scientist who has worked for many years on issues related to art categorization and authentication.[70] At present, their main customers, according to Popovici, are collectors, auction houses, and galleries.

Perhaps the most novel facet of the deep learning method that Art Recognition employs, as opposed to other methods of art authentication, is that they never need to physically examine the work. Customers can access their authentication services by sending in an ordinary photo of the work to receive a report from the company regarding its likely authenticity.[71] According to Popovici, "A photo taken with a last generation iPhone is okay, so the quality has to be good but not extraordinary." In other words, the photo needs to be a frontal view with no artifacts or light reflections but otherwise of normal snapshot quality—no fine details of the surface necessary. This photo is then compared to their database of authenticated works, which is gathered from "reliable online and offline sources" such as catalogue raisonnées and museum databases.[72]

The report that customers receive in return includes a percentage probability that the work is an original by the artist in question, a heat map visualization of the analysis, and information on the data used and model performance. The heat map shows, via hotspots represented in shades of red, areas that were of particular interest within the image in the determination of the work's authenticity. According to a sample report that Art Recognition has produced, which analyzes a fake Max Pechstein painting, *Seine mit Brücke und Frachtkränen* created by notorious forger Wolfgang Beltracchi, "These regions [marked as hotspots in the image] stem from the analysis of the readable brushstroke and other structural characteristics, and are not related to the artistic representation."[73] In other words, Art Recognition points out that their analysis has nothing to do with content of the image, but rather deals with elements of style and technique.

In an interview, Hoppe-Oehl states that Art Recognition sees their service as a tool that can add to rather than replace existing methods, becoming a "fourth pillar" of authentication alongside connoisseurship, provenance study, and chemical/material analysis.[74] Popovici reiterates this view, stating:

> We see our technology as complimentary to traditional authentication methods as each method has its advantages. If a forger doesn't use pigments and canvases from the period of the artist, he can be found out by laboratory analysis. If he doesn't invent a credible provenance

> or is not good at copying the style of an artist, the art expert will realize it quickly. But still many forgers succeed, and our tool can add an additional layer of certainty.[75]

Nevertheless, there are indications that deep learning techniques are already gaining acceptance in authenticity cases. According to an article in the *Economist*, European customs authorities deemed a certificate from Art Recognition as acceptable proof that a copy of an Impressionist painting was indeed not authentic.[76]

Still, not everyone is happy to accept Art Recognition's determination that a work is inauthentic. It seems that art experts accept the judgment of algorithms as long as they confirm what those experts already believe or if that judgment is in the best interest of the institution. For example, Art Recognition have also claimed that a painting attributed to Peter Paul Rubens in the National Gallery in London was not painted by the artist, but the museum stated that they would await further evidence and research.[77]

As is often the case when it comes to processes traditionally confined to human judgment that have been automated through deep learning, it is necessary to reassert that such processes do not have the ultimate say in decision making. Machine learning is thus positioned in a complementary relationship with human judgment or as a partnership.[78] Another tech start-up that has entered the scene is Artrendex, a company run by Ahmad Elgammal with products based on his academic research, which is discussed at length in chapter 1 of this book.[79] Artrendex provides three different AI-powered services geared toward the art market: AIPi, an art analytics product; AICAN, a "creative partner" in making art, discussed below; and Art Verified by AI, the authentication wing of the company. Like Art Recognition, Art Verified by AI seems to focus on analyzing digital image textures related to brushstrokes (or drawing strokes). In a publication from 2017, Elgammal and his collaborators outline how they used stroke analysis to authenticate and attribute drawings as created by Pablo Picasso or Henri Matisse, or determine that they are fake.[80] Their work draws inspiration from the methods of Dutch researcher M. M. van Dantzig (1903–1960), who developed a stroke-based method of connoisseurship in the mid-twentieth century.[81] According to a review of Van Dantzig's work from 1959, "He is convinced that, although the emotion created by art is purely subjective, the immediate cause of that emotion must be accessible to objective or at least inter-subjective appreciation."[82] Van Dantzig's methods have remained rather obscure since his death, until Netherlands-based researchers interested in both digital connoisseurship and creating an objective means of art authentication revived them in service of digital stroke-analysis techniques.[83] One article even goes so far as to claim that the use of computers negates criticism of Van Dantzig's aspirations toward objectivity.[84]

Still, some researchers are not wholly convinced of the widespread applicability of such techniques. In a publication from 2008, engineering professor C. Richard Johnson used a combination of machine learning methods including brushstroke analysis to analyze Van Gogh paintings.[85] In an interview a decade later, however, he points out a number of faults with the brushstroke approach. For one, he states that strokes are "rarely individualized" as they are in Elgammal's Matisse and Picasso line drawings. He also points out that brushstrokes can be invisible in some works or that artists' styles can change over time. He concludes that he is "quite skeptical" about the relative impact of such techniques.[86]

In addition to the fact that artistic style is rarely totally consistent and unchanging over the course of a long career, the medium and materials an artist uses can significantly alter how the strokes in the work appear. Different types of paper and different drawing materials (ink, brush, crayon, charcoal, etc.) are two factors that Elgammal and colleagues cite as challenges to their brushstroke analysis methods.[87] Making matters more difficult is that artists do not distribute their work equally among media. So even within the already strict confines of line drawings, one might have to compare ink drawings to charcoal drawings, which produce fundamentally different types of strokes.

Additionally, the quality of the digital images can significantly affect how the brushstrokes are quantified at the level of pixels. Differences in luminance for different digitized images can change the readings of the brushstrokes as well. In existing implementations of machine learning, both with handcrafted features and with learned features, researchers tend to use lower resolution and compositionally abstracted or cropped images because they perform better (and process more quickly) than higher resolution images. Images are drawn from a variety of sources in order to avoid categorization by type or source of digital image as opposed to content or composition *within* the image. As the SIFT technique described in the introduction to this book demonstrates, too many details can muddle pattern recognition and make categorization too noisy. This element of machine learning, in its current manifestations, seems at odds with the highly detailed analysis of artworks that human connoisseurs perform. Once again, therefore, we cannot discount differences in digitization as a key factor to address when authentication techniques use digital images in lieu of the actual works in comparison studies.[88]

Given that the inconsistencies and unevenness of art datasets can be accommodated in brushstroke analysis, there are other issues regarding the input data that might be more difficult to recognize or address using such processes. This is an issue, once again, of "garbage in, garbage out." How much art do we *think* is authentic but is actually fake? That is, what about tainted datasets? The former director of the Metropolitan Museum of Art, Thomas Hoving, once claimed that 40% of the work in art museums is fake. Likewise, Yann Walther, the head of the Swiss Fine Art Experts Institute claimed that it is a conservative estimate that at least 50% of the work circulating in the art market is fake or misattributed.[89] How can algorithmic methods be trusted if the datasets themselves are not reliable?

Each piece of the authentication puzzle has potential pitfalls. Laboratory analysis of materials can detect only whether the materials themselves are anachronistic, which is a hurdle forgers can overcome by sourcing period-specific materials and using those to make their fakes. Machine learning methods rely on digital images and new, cutting-edge techniques that have not been significantly tested yet. And human experts are likely to let their emotions or financial interests sway them in one way or another. Considering all these factors, it might be tempting to say that authentication always was and will always be a largely unknowable puzzle. Indeed, in many cases it might well be. This is why, typically, those who are serious about authentication will use a combination of several different methods before making a judgment.

In evaluating the relationship between traditional Morellian connoisseurship and emerging digital methods of authentication, some researchers have argued that such methods are still no replacement for human evaluators in that humans have culpability for the decisions that they make. In the process of their research, which, as noted, attempts to implement

Morelli's method using machine learning techniques, Langmead and colleagues realized the ultimate fallibility of computational systems in the realm of judgment. As with the importation of other methods from the sciences into humanities research, computational analysis has been accompanied by claims of objectivity that fall apart under scrutiny. They write, "We came to recognize that what truly lies at the heart of a successful (or failed) art attribution is not simply endorsing the accuracy of formal comparisons, but the ability to participate in a community of trusted experts and to take full responsibility for one's own inferences and judgments."[90] Although it may be true that trusting the supposed scientific objectivity of either Morelli's system or a computational version of it fails to acknowledge that "art attribution is a practice fully embedded in sociality," the repeated human failings of experts detailed above provide culpability but little else. The numerous instances in which human experts have been compromised by the same sociality that Langmead and colleagues praise indicate that art historians and collectors cannot put too much faith in the social element either.[91]

Inherent in these discussions of human judgment versus machinic certainty is the lingering question of whether truth should have any place at all in humanities research today. Assigning some percentage of numerical accuracy has never been part of the process of art-historical research. This does not mean that art history eschews facts and evidence, but rather that such things are used in the service of persuasion rather than numerical probability or prediction. Regardless of whether academic art historians take up questions of authenticity, however, the art market will continue to search for increased levels of certainty regarding the attribution of artworks. The market, after all, is based on both probability and prediction, and the more certainty art authentication experts can provide, the more money can potentially be made.

Next-Level Forgeries and Fakes

As researchers invent new ways to detect fakes and forgeries in the art world, art forgers adapt in turn and learn from the very same techniques that are used to catch them. This has been described as the "arms race" of art authentication.[92] This is true not only for the chemical and material analysis of art forgeries but may well be true for the use of deep learning techniques in the future. If deep learning can detect fake art, why can it not provide information to help create fake art in the first place?

One of the most exciting—and troubling—applications of machine learning in recent years is creative or generative AI, in which deep learning algorithms are used to create new media (text, video, images, and audio) on the basis of training data. Two of the most commonly cited techniques for image creation are generative adversarial networks (GANs), described in a publication from 2014, and variational autoencoders (VAEs), first described in 2013.[93] There are also numerous image creation projects like DALL-E and Midjourney, which became popular among a wider public in 2022, that use generative models to create images from text prompts.[94]

The projects discussed in this chapter mostly use variations of GAN. Simply put, GANs consist of two models, a generator and a discriminator. If, for example, the GAN were set up to create new images, the generator would propose plausible images created from what it "learned" from a given training dataset, and the discriminator would determine whether these images could pass for what already exists in the database. This play back and forth is the "adversarial" part of the system, which allows a process of refining to happen. This process can produce striking results, such as in the work of Karras and colleagues, who produced highly believable computer-generated faces using a GAN system.[95] A website based on their work, https://thispersondoesnotexist.com, presents some examples of these images, which appear to be the faces of real people but are in fact completely constructed.

Generative models have raised particular alarm in the media with regard to so-called deepfakes, videos that are seamlessly altered to appear to show people saying things that they never said or doing all sorts of things that they never did.[96] For example, this technology has seen applications in politics, where politicians and world leaders can be made to say anything the deepfake creator wants them to, and pornography, where celebrities' faces are seamlessly sutured onto pornographic performers' bodies.[97]

Returning to the question of art, however, artists and researchers have increasingly turned to deep learning to create new works, using deep learning techniques on images of existing works from a certain artist or group of artists. Although no one has yet—as far as we know—created a forgery based on machine learning that was then passed off as authentic in the art market, there have been a number of experiments in creating new works in the style of Old Masters. These experiments typically aim not only to understand the broad trends in how a particular set of paintings are constructed—on the basis of subject matter, composition, color, and so on—but also to reproduce them. The result is a distillation, composite, or statistical sampling of the group, as interpreted through the processing layers.

One example of this is The Next Rembrandt, a project unveiled by Microsoft in 2016 in collaboration with ING bank, Delft University of Technology, Mauritshuis, and the Rijksmuseum.[98] The idea of the project was to create a completely new "Rembrandt" painting based on analysis of his existing paintings and produced with a 3D printer. The researchers used techniques to analyze a number of different aspects of the paintings, including the subject matter (including facial recognition) and the surface depth/texture of the works. It is this last step—capturing data on the materiality of a Rembrandt painting—that sets the project apart from many other deep learning applications in art. 3D printing may not be a particularly precise method of recreating the brushstrokes or texture of an artwork, but there are plenty of efforts in the realm of robotics that attempt to more precisely mimic brushstroke data, which one could foresee applied in future art forgeries.[99]

In distilling Rembrandt's work, the Microsoft team decided to make the subject of their new painting the most commonly represented one within Rembrandt's oeuvre: a portrait of a white male with facial hair, 30–40 years old, wearing a hat and dark clothing with a collar, and facing to the right. The visibility of the input data bias that this subject represents was evidently of little interest to Microsoft and its researchers, even in passing. We can assume that the researchers just let the data "speak for itself" in providing the suggested subject, a generic seventeenth-century white male. In a case such as this, concerning something relatively trivial—a portrait of a hypothetical Rembrandt subject, the output of the project pretty clearly displays the values of the society from which the data was gathered, seventeenth-century Holland. However, these societal biases represented in the output of deep learning experiments may not be so starkly presented when data is allowed to "speak for itself" in other contexts, such as policing or surveillance. So, although I would not argue that the subject matter of the new Rembrandt work need be anything other than what the Microsoft team chose, a reflection on what it represents, which moves beyond data divination, is certainly warranted.

Unsurprisingly, perhaps, the new Rembrandt did not meet widespread praise from art experts. Critiquing the project from the perspective of connoisseurship, Ernst van de Wetering pointed out what he saw as obvious faults in the stylistic details of the "painting." Other critics objected to the work on the grounds that it failed to exhibit the human sentiment or meaning underpinning great works of art.[100] Tsila Hassine and Ziv Neeman, on the other hand, label the Next Rembrandt project as an example of "Zombie Art," and compare it unfavorably to nondigital forgery techniques, asserting that "the human forger injects at least a modicum of creativity to the forgery."[101] I believe that this is a romanticization of forgers' creativity, however, which lies primarily in the narratives they spin around themselves and their work rather than genuine artistic innovation, which would surely defeat the purpose of producing a convincing fake.[102]

Contrary to the naysayers, Luciano Floridi calls the Microsoft Rembrandt a "masterpiece," due to its uniquely unoriginal nature. He labels this type of work an *ectype*: "a copy, yet not any copy, but rather a copy that has a special relation with its source."[103] It is this last point, I would argue, that gets closest to the heart of how AI-created works operate and what stakes are involved. Works such as this are metarepresentations.

As noted, photographic compositing has a dark history. In the nineteenth century, composited photographs were used by figures such as Francis Galton among others to determine generalized criminal and ethnic "types." An AI-generated portrait can also be considered a type of composite image in that it draws its form from a multitude of images to create a new, single image that shares characteristics with these multiple sources. Although not all composites directly embody prejudiced ideologies, the act of compositing erases individual specificity in favor of an imagined stereotype. Whereas GAN is a far more complex process than simple photographic compositing, the algorithm cannot create anything truly new that is not related to the input that it is given. So, although the algorithm *does* create a completely new (and often unexpected) image, this image is always related in some way to the contents of the database.

In order to create the "new" Rembrandt portrait, the Microsoft researchers also worked to isolate facial features from the existing Rembrandt portraits to analyze and reproduce. In doing so, they implicitly provide an interpretation of art in which the individual people or context depicted in portraits are of no subsequent importance. The artist's fame and master style trumps context completely. Remnants of culture, such as facial hair and stiff white collars or all-black attire, become incidental rather than essential. The technique is reminiscent of Morelli's method in that eyes, ears, noses, and other facial features are supposed to provide a unified style of facial representation, regardless of the appearance of the portrait's sitter.

AN ARTIFICIAL ARTIST?

The application of creative AI in future art forgeries is pure speculation at this point, and The Next Rembrandt project, although close in concept to a forgery, remained relatively far away from one in terms of its execution. There are, however, other examples of creative AI experiments that have generated new artworks less explicitly tied to the oeuvre of one artist, which nevertheless follow a similar trajectory of distilling Old Masters and the historical genre of portraiture into something new. The first example is from a group of French artists called the Obvious collective. This portrait was sold at Christie's in 2018 for $432,500. It is one of a group of portraits of a fictional Belamy family that the group created. The second example is from Elgammal and his research associates, who produced a series of AI-assisted portraits with the aforementioned AICAN. The results of Elgammal's experiments were exhibited at a contemporary art gallery in Chelsea, New York, and received widespread media coverage in both the art and the technology press.[104]

These two examples are noteworthy in that both projects have garnered a lot of media attention and were both initiated by nonartists or untrained artists from a position outside of the art world. Both also double as creative AI businesses, which differentiates them from the myriad of artists working with machine learning and creative AI in a critical way today.[105] Trevor Paglen, whose work in collaboration with Kate Crawford is discussed in chapter 1 of this book, is one example of an artist who is actively engaged with machine learning and creative AI. His work dealing with bias in machine learning systems grows out of a larger body of working investigating systems of surveillance enabled by digital technology.[106]

Another artist who has been working with creative AI applications is Ian Cheng, whose piece *BOB* (2018–2019), which stands for "bag of beliefs" (a riff on the "bag of words" model for machine learning), is an AI creature that learns, metabolizes, and "dies many deaths."[107] Meanwhile, artist Stephanie Dinkins has used deep learning in works like *Not the Only One* (2017), which is a system designed to create a "multigenerational memoir of a black American family" via a learning algorithm that has been trained on oral histories.[108] In yet another critical application of machine learning, the art collective Forensic Architecture's piece *Triple-Chaser* (2019) used automated image classifiers to comb through a large number of photos from the United States–Mexico border to identify tear gas canisters used against migrants. They wanted to identify canisters produced by Safariland, a company owned by Warren B. Kanders, the former vice chair of the board of trustees of the Whitney Museum of American Art in New York.[109] Their efforts ultimately became part of a successful campaign to get Kanders to step down from the Whitney board.[110]

Projects such as these, as well as others that are too numerous to describe here, explore and use machine learning and computer vision techniques in order to comment and reflect on philosophical or social issues in the context of contemporary art. As such, none of them represent deep connoisseurship in the way that Obvious and AICAN's projects do. For these latter projects, the extraction and learning from formal details of historical paintings, particularly portraiture, are taken as the sole markers or criteria for creating new works of art. There is also an element of publicity seeking and gimmick in both of these examples that calls into question whether we can or should seriously engage with these works or the grand statements that Obvious or Elgammal have made to accompany them.

Obvious was formed by three French students, Hugo Caselles-Dupré, Pierre Fautrel, and Gauthier Vernier, inspired by the work of artist and programmer Robbie Barrat. Shortly after the advent of GAN in 2014, Barrat published code for his own GAN art experiments on GitHub for anyone to use, and Obvious borrowed heavily from this.[111] The *Edmond de Belamy* portrait that they sold at Christie's was created using fifteen thousand images from WikiArt dated between the fourteenth and nineteenth centuries. Caselles-Dupré, who often acts as spokesperson for the group, said of the portrait, "Think of it as the 15,001st image."[112] Much like The Next

Rembrandt, the result is a portrait of a white man dressed in somber black clothing, although with less precise facial detail than Microsoft's project. As part of the publicity push ahead of the auction, Obvious made a number of sweeping statements attributing all responsibility for the art to the "creativity" of the algorithm. They even signed the portrait with the formula of the loss function of the original GAN model.[113]

Although Caselles-Dupré later backtracked on some of the broader claims that Obvious had made at the time of the auction that seemed to suggest algorithmic autonomy in the creation of the work, his statements around creativity are nevertheless worth interrogating.[114] Caselles-Dupré explained the group's choice of portraiture, saying, "We did some work with nudes and landscapes, and we also tried feeding the algorithm sets of works by famous painters. But we found that portraits provided the best way to illustrate our point, which is that algorithms are able to emulate creativity."[115] In other words, Caselles-Dupré seems to suggest that perhaps the most highly standardized genre of traditional Western art is the form within which GAN can truly show its creative potential. The philosophical discourse around artificial creativity can be fraught, as it often leads back to more general debates around the nature of creativity itself, as a concept. Likewise, discussions around art created through AI systems raise questions about what constitutes and defines art and creativity more generally.[116]

It is therefore fair to say, despite the hype around computational autonomy, that the creator of the system that produces art using AI is responsible for both its status as art and its potential creativity. Caselles-Dupré admits as much, stating that people working with GANs are essentially "curating data sets."[117] However, as with the feature visualizations already discussed, what we are faced with in Obvious's work is an interpretation of what the system has extrapolated as common (we might interpret this as meaningful or important) features in Western portraiture: a white, vaguely male face turned to the side, black clothing and a white collar on a neutral background. This, like The Next Rembrandt, is a product of deep connoisseurship, and it is therefore not so far-fetched to see it as a kind of algorithmic forgery of Western art.

The AICAN project similarly used Western painting to create a series of *Faceless Portraits Transcending Time*, as the exhibition title at HG Contemporary in New York (February 12–March 5, 2019) labeled them.[118] The works shown were even less guided toward naturalism than The Next Rembrandt or *Edmond de Belamy*. These faceless subjects are still recognizable as derived from historical portraits of people but are highly abstracted in the now-familiar style of algorithmically generated images, in which distorted or doubled elements or features of the source material are composited and melt into fleshy, incongruous globules. This melting, eerie, or uncanny quality of GAN imagery has often seen it compared to the Surrealist movement of the early twentieth century. This superficial relationship is perhaps one of the reasons why Elgammal has claimed that his AICAN system effectively demonstrates a modernist art-historical teleology, proving that art is formally deterministic. He states:

> An interesting question is: why is so much of the CAN's art abstract? I think it is because the algorithm has grasped that art progresses in a certain trajectory. If it wants to make something novel, then it cannot go back and produce figurative works as existed before the 20th century. It has to move forward. The network has learned that it finds more solutions when it tends toward abstraction: that is where there is the space for novelty.[119]

Briefly put, this kind of statement raises alarm bells not only because of the *intentionality* that Elgammal seems to attribute to the AICAN system but because he uses this supposed sentience to make a specious argument about art's "progress" toward abstraction. This modernist concept has, of course, been thoroughly debunked and unraveled over the last half century. As discussed, one of the main reasons for this is the contradiction that universalism presents when faced with the scope and breadth of art traditions outside of Western art history.

One of the key facets of all these projects is their decision to produce "portraits." As Ian Bogost has pointed out in the case of AICAN, this seems to misunderstand the intrinsic point of interest in historical oil portraiture.[120] The assumption that Elgammal and his group make is that they are distilling the best "innovation" from a number of masterpieces, even though one of the key centers of meaning for portraiture is the historical specificity of the time period, the artist, and those depicted. The fact that thousands of portraits are analyzed by the AI system before it can create a "new" one raises the question of whether such works can indeed be termed portraits at all, as they are absent of these contextual markers of portraiture.

In an essay on the Fayum portraits of the first to third century—Egyptian tomb paintings—John Berger writes that the immediacy that these portraits present to the viewer is due to their purpose in funeral rituals and the fact that they were not meant to be seen again after death. These were not idealized portraits, but rather direct representations of the faces of the dead designed to identify them in the afterlife. For this reason, Berger calls them "passport photos," writing, "To paint was to name."[121] What, then, is the meaning of not only compressing the portraits of thousands of people into a single "new" image but also thousands of different points in time in which those images were painted? We lose the immediacy; we lose the individuality of both the sitter and the artist.

Elgammal writes that his exhibition "transcends time," but what it does is create a soup of time in which the viewer loses each image's historical and formal specificity, not unlike the amorphous soup of features in the portraits themselves. I would argue that this is the primary reason that these images are relevant to art history—their soupy form—not their expression of autonomous creativity. Human and machinic "choices" were made in the creation of all three examples: The Next Rembrandt, *Edmond de Belamy*, and AICAN's faceless portraits. However, they are not mathematical proofs of art-historical fact nor are they functionally independent of the curatorial decisions made by the computer scientists responsible for them. The formal soup of the images created using deep learning is both a new way of representing time and a new way of seeing. While novel, it is also strikingly consistent. Once one has seen enough deep learning-created images, the same facets of representation repeatedly appear. The glib addition of a formula in lieu of a signature on Obvious's *Edmond de Belamy* is therefore very misleading. The formula is, in fact, written all over the image itself. It is not the author, but rather the tool and the subject. All these portraits are, first and foremost, portraits of the process itself.

In cleaving to and deriving from connoisseurship via the use of historical art images, however, these examples of AI portraiture could easily be defined primarily as art forgeries—those works that pretend to be new or until-recently-undiscovered masterpieces of the past—rather than "originals." Indeed, if they were created using any other methods besides computational ones, would they even be discussed in the context of originality and creativity? The digital era has presented many challenges to traditional ideas about the value of art in the Western world, which has long prized originality and individual craft. As this chapter has shown, however, deep learning presents additional wrinkles to contemporary discussions of value and authenticity in art.

POOR IMAGES

In his work *Eye/Machine* (2001), filmmaker Harun Farocki (1944–2014) coined the term "operative images" to describe a type of image that is "part of an operation," that is, not intended for human viewing, but rather designed for machine viewing or analysis.[122] Farocki's work in the 2000s explored such images in the realm of surveillance, war, factories, shopping, entertainment, and other facets of modern life. Trevor Paglen, reflecting on the use of operative (aka operational) images in 2014, wrote, "Increasingly, operational images are not simply alien to humans—they are literally invisible."[123] This is even more relevant today, as black box deep learning has come to dominate the field of computer vision.

Art authentication, as determined by artistic style, requires that art images be treated as operative images. As is the case in many of the settings that Farocki addressed in his work, such as government or industry, human viewership in art is no longer the only or the most trusted authority in making determinations regarding attribution. Just as earlier computer vision research produced methods that are now entrusted to sort different kind of screws in an assembly line (and do so more quickly and accurately than a human sorter could), contemporary machine learning is increasingly being entrusted with the task of sorting artworks. Computer vision, not unlike Morelli's methods of connoisseurship in the nineteenth century, ignores the aspects of an artwork that a human might find interesting, such as the narrative, theme, or overarching composition, and instead breaks down the work into a "bag of features" to analyze. In other words, as representations of artworks transition in status to operative images, they become further and further unmoored from context.

These operative art images have a similar status to the type of images that artist Hito Steyerl has termed "poor images."[124] In her "defense of the poor image," Steyerl, who counts Farocki as a strong influence on her work, defines poor images as the low-resolution, quickly moving images that often populate the internet. What separates these images from their high-quality cousins is their detachment—and therefore freedom—from context in lieu of speed, flexibility, and permutability. She writes, "The poor image is an illicit fifth-generation bastard of an original image. Its genealogy is dubious. . . . It often defies patrimony, national culture, or indeed copyright. It is passed on as a lure, a decoy, an index, or as a reminder of its former visual self."[125] Essentially, poor images are copies that have shed their provenance.

This tension between the copy and the original permeates deep connoisseurship. On one hand, deep connoisseurship flips many of the traditional assumptions regarding authenticity around: instead of revolving around the unique qualities of an individual work, authenticity revolves around mass comparison, using thousands of digital copies; instead of requiring high resolution, it often functions better when the source material is downscaled, altered, or abstracted to avoid the "noise" of too much detail. On the other hand, deep connoisseurship carries on the traditions of Morellian connoisseurship in its fragmentation of artworks and the way that attribution is "diagnosed" in relation to these fragments rather than in relation to an understanding of the whole.

The poor images used to authenticate artworks are therefore paradoxical. From a certain perspective, their definition as lures that are pirated, appropriated, and passed off in place of their originals puts these poor art images in league with the art fakes and forgeries that they are meant to expose. From a different perspective, however, they "create a new aura" that is "no longer based on the permanence of the 'original,' but on the transience of the copy."[126] In other words, processed and manipulated shadows and fragments of artworks, which have a dubious relationship to traditional notions of authenticity, have become the basis upon which the authenticity of artworks is determined. The original is no longer needed. That is, deep connoisseurship splits the concepts of authenticity and originality apart. Against all odds, the poor images have inherited the earth.

3

Conclusion: Man, Machine, Metaphor

On July 20, 1969, the first humans landed on the moon as part of the Apollo 11 mission. One often-told narrative in the wake of the mission was that, when the lunar module was nearing its landing target, a program alarm went off and the computer began to reboot. Astronaut Neil Armstrong was then forced to turn off the computer and safely land the vehicle manually, seeming to have demonstrated the superiority of man versus machine. In concluding this book, which highlights some of the confluence and conflicts between art history and data science, I see the story of Apollo 11 as a metaphor for interdisciplinarity. So often, collaborations between qualitative and quantitative research set up a relationship of "man versus machine," but on reflection, it is far more fruitful to think about the relationship as that of "man *in* the machine," neither fully mechanized nor fully humanized.

The Apollo 11 narrative of human triumph and machinic unreliability played well into the American ideological agenda of the time. It became part of the greater narrative of American rugged individualism and pioneer spirit, portraying the astronaut as the cowboy, the master of *his* own destiny. For the Americans, the astronaut was not a cog in a communal state machine, but an independent individual who would not be rationalized or engineered through modern technology. The ideological narrative of Apollo, which conveniently omits the essential work of teams of hardware and software developers, speaks not only to the politics of the time but reflects a broader distrust of complex computational tools that persists today. Both at the time of Apollo 11 and today, in the age of machine learning, gut instinct and craft are held up to be more human and therefore reliable. Rather than scientific knowledge and craft being interrelated, working together in tandem, the old trope of man *versus* machine is reinforced and the distinct humanness of the system is unacknowledged.

In the book *Digital Apollo*, David A. Mindell investigates the engineering and computer systems that aided the success of the Apollo space program.[1] In an interview, he recounts the reaction to the story of Apollo 11's computer failure:

> As I began doing the research on the book and I talked to the engineers who built that computer, they were all highly offended by that version of the story. They felt that there had been a problem that had been actually caused by the astronauts following a checklist that was in error. And the computer had done all kinds of wonderful things in order to save the mission. And the real bug in the system overall was not in a piece of computer code, but it was a bug in the complex human organizational system on the ground that created this very rich, complicated technology.[2]

Whichever way one looks at it, whether it is the human or the machine that is believed to be superior in this scenario, the *versus* relationship remains.

In the subsequent six Apollo missions, astronauts found similar reasons to take over manual control of the spacecraft. The pilots-turned-astronauts felt that they had a valuable skill as pilots and that their ability to judge and sensorially perceive their surroundings placed them in a superior position when it came to landing on the moon. They did not want to become "spam in a can," little more than cargo, and let an automated computer system guide their path. The reality, however, was that the moon landing was achieved through cooperation. It was a joint effort to create hardware, software, and trained operators—human and machine inextricably intertwined.

In 1967, conceptual artist Sol LeWitt said, "The idea becomes the machine that makes the art." Systems art and many types of conceptual art employ programmatic thinking, proposing a series of directives to be followed or completed. Although they do not necessarily make use of literal computers, they nevertheless utilize the logic and language of systems, computing and programming. It is not a coincidence that artists were inspired by systems theory in the 1960s. As Michael Corris argues,

> The concept of a "system," which became part of the *lingua franca* of the 1960s, was not destined to remain the exclusive property of a

> technologically minded elite of engineers, scientists and mathematicians. In the hands of intellectuals, artists and political activists, it would become a key ideological component of the "cultural revolution."[3]

People began to understand themselves as part of a myriad of systems—political, social, and cultural. What might have initially been seen as a corruption of engineering principles is now an intrinsic part of how the broader shape of society is understood. Social *systems* are a metaphor more than a reality; they provide a neat concept for understanding the complexity of human organizational structures, in which the component parts are positioned as necessary actors in the function of the whole. If one of these component parts is faulty, the social system fails.

Systems artists embraced the rationalism and neatness of programmatic thinking as a way to reflect on whether the role of the artist is more pilot or engineer, to use the dichotomy set up by the Apollo mission. Ultimately, artists, creators, and thinkers are always both. One of the major points of criticism that systems and conceptual art faced was that there is no skill or craft involved. By seeming to discard skill—which is at the etymological root of artistic practice—it abandoned the most "human" of all pursuits. This was never a question of either/or, however. On the contrary, much of systems and conceptual art reveals the entanglement of the man in the machine. It embraced the system—but as a metaphor.

In order to understand the human mind, both scientists and the public tend to use metaphor. More often than not, these metaphors are a reflection of the technology and/or dominant beliefs of any given period in history.[4] In recent times, the brain as a computer has become the dominant metaphor. Thoughts are *processed*, information is *retrieved*, memories are *stored*. Computational neural networks like those discussed in this book are, in a way, a reverse of this common computer-mind metaphor: the computer is thought of as a human brain rather than the brain as a computer. Thus, the computer-mind metaphor has become something of a tautology: the computer can be understood as a brain and the brain as a computer despite the fact that they are not generally thought of as equivalent. This can mean that computers are humanized and people dehumanized; the computer is brought to life and the human demoted to fleshy automaton. Fear of dehumanization or human obsolescence lies at the heart of the opposition between man and machine.

The technology that facilitates space travel, both hardware and software, embodies the potential distance between what the human body alone can do versus what technology stretches it to do. Simple tools, such as a pencil, seem relatively safe. We have no fear that pencils will overtake humans because they remain close to our bodies and they augment our ability to write but do not do so to such an extent that the body's movement is abstracted beyond recognition. The pencil responds to commands of the brain telling the fingers to control it. Once we automate this process, however, it starts to feel threatening. Once it requires several people rather than an individual to create the program, it begins to feel even more threatening. Somehow this machine acquires the power of a community of people rather than the individual intellect of the lone human being. Collaboration introduces scale and the sublime fear that entails.

Deep learning systems often function as black boxes, meaning that we do not know the inner "thought process" through which the system arrives at its output. Although researchers are now studying how the inner workings of these black boxes might be visualized or otherwise explained, there are still many applications of deep learning that remain opaque, even to their creators. This may seem like we have relinquished control to the machine, but in reality these systems can work only with the input given to them—the data. To quote Andrew G. Ferguson again, "Data is us, just reduced to binary code."[5] Often, data is many, many, many of us—so many that we may forget that it is a representation of the collective, albeit a very large collective.

The fear of artificial intelligence or the battle of man versus machine somehow boils down to the fear that no single person can compete with or against the automated product of communal activity. All academic research disciplines, however, have always fluctuated between communal and individual achievement, neither of which is more or less human. Digital humanists often argue that quantitative methods allow researchers to "read" and compare thousands (or even millions) more books or artworks than they would otherwise be able to. As noted, however, Nan Z. Da argues that this ignores the cumulative and collaborative nature of traditional humanities research in which masses of material are already collaboratively analyzed, through the readings and accumulated knowledge of many, many researchers.[6]

The term "artificial intelligence" is laden with baggage. Whereas it may describe a specific area of computer science research, it has long been compromised by both utopian and dystopian fantasies. Much like the example of systems and conceptual art above, the fear for humanists is that the application of so-called artificial intelligence in humanities disciplines removes the human from the equation. What are we left with then? It is for this reason that any such discussions need to recognize the human origins, biases, and drivers in any quantitative system, especially those labeled as artificial intelligence. Instead of sentient machines devoid of the human biases or individual failures that may color traditional humanities methods, they should be seen as augmented—albeit abstracted and distant—human thought or gesture that unites cumulative craft and knowledge. In other words, we might look at the relationship between the humanities and the technical sciences not as a question of man versus machine but as a question of the man in the machine.

There is a long history of human competition with machinic creations leading up to the Apollo 11 story. Amazon's piecework system, Mechanical Turk, takes its name from one of the most famous early examples of an automaton competing against human opponents. The original Mechanical Turk was a chess-playing automaton that toured the royal courts of Europe in the eighteenth century, competing against and besting human competitors along the way. The machine was later revealed to be a hoax, however—an actual human chess player was hiding inside it, working the mechanisms. Amazon's system is aptly named, then, as it "contains" the thousands of workers whose labor power is necessary to make many of the automated or artificial intelligence systems of today function.

Viewed from this perspective, automation functions more as a metaphor than a reality. Yes, there are processes that actually proceed automatically, many of which have been profiled in this book. Some even proceed in wholly unknown or unexpected ways, as is the case in many deep learning experiments. However, each of these automated processes is based on human input and data curation/creation. To a lesser or greater extent, there is always a man in the machine.

The aim of this book has been to address a body of research in computer science that introduces new machine learning methodologies for the analysis of artworks. This research has, until now, received little attention from the academic discipline(s) devoted to the study of art, art history, and visual studies. In the past decade, more and more studies analyzing images of artworks have been published in the fields of machine learning and computer vision. These studies approach art from a very different perspective from that of most art historians. Given this, I set out to analyze a sampling of this area of research from an art historian's perspective, tracing the relationship between these new methods and the historiographic traditions of the discipline. The implication of doing so reasserts the presence of the man in the machine as described above. In other words, the preceding chapters demystify the human role in both creation and analysis of artworks as data in recent machine learning applications. The supposed lack of humanity in quantitative research is held up as both a virtue and a serious failing, but the reality is that humans and humanist issues are present in such methods every step of the way: from the analog repositories or collections of artworks to their digitization, from data creation/curation to metadata, and from the development of algorithms/computational processes to their eventual interpretation.

Although the hybrid field of digital art history borrows from the methods developed in computer science, it has struggled to maintain a connection to the humanist methods at the core of its mother discipline, art history. One of the side effects of putting computational methods under an art-historical lens is that art history methods and practice are, in turn, called into question. The first chapter of this book looked at the unremarked bias and issues of art datasets used by computer science researchers, particularly in their labeling of period/movement style and analysis by that parameter. The faults in this, however, do not originate with unwitting computer scientists, but rather are rooted in a much longer history. The discipline of art history has struggled for decades to understand and rectify the dominance of a certain version of the Western canon of art. However, as it is defined through existing museum collections and art historians alike, the canon has become an unshakeable monolith and part of the global brand of Western art. The second chapter of this book likewise looks at how deep learning is applied in artwork identification, particularly in cases of authentication and forgery. Although academic art historians are often keen to ignore the long shadow of the art market over the discipline, the application of machine learning techniques to this arena places a spotlight on how value and authenticity are continually redefined and propped up by museums and art historians alike.

The question that remains, then, is how to proceed in interdisciplinary research so that a genuine interface of communication is established across the epistemological divide. As it stands in digital art history, methods are typically ceded to computer science and subject matter to art history. Alternatively, computational methods are presented as a starting point and humanist interpretation is layered thereafter. The university discipline of art history began as a positivist, taxonomy-obsessed discipline. In its over one hundred years of existence, however, it has evolved to incorporate a variety of critiques to its initial formulation and has supplemented existing methodologies with a body of critical frameworks for analyzing works of art and material culture. Whereas the positivist and taxonomical aspects of art history have never gone away, they have waned considerably in importance over the last fifty years. How do we bridge the methodological gap?

THE RISE OF THE HUMANITIES LAB

The lab is the symbol and embodiment of research in the natural sciences, and its introduction into humanities research has created discomfort and debate among humanists. As discussed in the introduction to this book, the use of computational methods for the study of culture has been popularized over the past decade under the banner of the digital humanities (DH). Given the diverging skill sets often required for such research, many projects are conducted by teams consisting of humanists and data/computer scientists. This has led to the creation of digital humanities labs at universities all over the world. For DH acolytes, this is where the interdisciplinary magic happens. But is the "humanities lab" an oxymoron?

In traditional humanities departments, coauthorship is still rare, let alone authorship among half a dozen to a dozen collaborators (as is common in the sciences). Although all scholarship functions as a collaborative endeavor, humanities scholarship maintains the illusion that it is a solitary pursuit. Or, as Brian Greenspan terms it, "the monastic myth of the isolated (tenured) scholar as ideal."[7] Likewise, Geoffrey Rockwell and Stéfan Sinclair contrast their computational methods with the those of Descartes—a stand-in for traditional humanities methods—in order "to confront the privilege of solitary reflection in academic practice."[8] The ongoing debates over methodological choices in the humanities, in which this book will certainly enter, often boil down to a competition over which methods are more progressive. Digital humanists will point to new technology as a progressive force in humanities disciplines, whereas critics claim that their complicity with business interests and managerial thinking is in fact a reactionary force that quashes criticality.[9]

The funding of digital humanities labs has elicited concern that universities no longer value the traditional methods of humanities researchers, which do not generally require huge budgets, complex equipment, and additional support staff. For instance, Daniel Allington, Sarah Brouillette, and David Golumbia take direct aim at the idea that humanities scholarship should be project- or lab-based. They argue:

> What Digital Humanities is *not* about, despite its explicit claims, is the use of digital or quantitative methodologies to answer research questions in the humanities. It is, instead, about the promotion of project-based learning and lab-based research over reading and writing, the rebranding of insecure campus employment as an empowering "alt-ac" career choice, and the redefinition of technical expertise as a form (indeed, the superior form) of humanist knowledge.[10]

These scholars make many valid points about the politics involved in promoting digital humanities initiatives and the types of labor valorized within such collaborations. However, in their characterization, the old Cold War propaganda stereotype that collective work is communist and individual achievements are capitalist has been turned around. Labs and collaborative labor are positioned as facets of neoliberal capitalism and individual, traditional scholarship is a force for the political Left.

Nevertheless, many humanists see collaboration as a positive development. It allows researchers to explore topics beyond their limited expertise and skill set and to communicate to a wider audience. For digital humanities projects, automation offers humanists the ability to sort through material in new ways. Given the high level of specialization among academic disciplines, however, bringing researchers from different fields together is not always a harmonious affair. There may be no middle ground when conflicting norms in academic culture and approach present themselves.

Digital humanities initiatives are often praised for their interdisciplinarity. However, the assumption that digital humanities research is interdisciplinary by default has been questioned by Tanya Clement.[11] She argues that it is more useful to think of interdisciplinarity as a situated practice rather than an all-seeing, all-knowing mastering of disciplines or metadisciplinary perspective. Art historian Koenraad Brosens, on the other hand, contends that terms like "interdisciplinary" and "multidisciplinary" have outgrown their usefulness in their ubiquity:

> Not only has their meaning been depleted by years of (ab)(mis)use, they also suggest that a domain expert (the art historian) should also be an expert . . . in other fields . . . the data and knowledge (r)evolution that started in the 1980s makes it difficult, if not impossible, for most researchers to become and remain an expert (even an expert *light*) in more than one field.[12]

Even if this assessment—that expertise in multiple fields is impossible—is overly pessimistic, the fact remains that contemporary academia is not set up for collaboration. Despite administrative push toward interdisciplinarity, researchers may not truly have the opportunity to operate in multiple disciplines until they have long been active in their field. Ideally, interdisciplinary work would start at the undergraduate or, at the latest, the doctoral level. However, truly interdisciplinary programs are still rare and often struggle to be taken seriously by purists in established disciplines.

Keeping criticism of the term "interdisciplinary" in mind, the humanities lab—if not an oxymoron—is nothing like a traditional academic research lab, which tends to stick to a specialized field shared by all the researchers involved. The humanities lab is, instead, built on interdisciplinarity. By characterizing the humanities lab as an instrument of governmental or corporate influence in academia, the implication is that research at such labs is rigid and utilitarian. The reality is that humanities labs often are defined by the lab as a metaphor rather than strict physical reality. This means that researchers are not always actively engaged shoulder to shoulder working at the DH equivalent of lab benches, but rather that the lab is a signifier of the desire to *experiment*.

FOREIGN METAPHORS AS INTERDISCIPLINARY TOOL

Humanities labs may be the site of interdisciplinary collaboration—but what, then, are the tools? What academic language is spoken? Critics have asserted that the humanities are methodologically subservient to the digital in DH projects.[13] In this scenario, humanists are forced the speak the language of computing, whereas computer scientists avoid the language of humanists. It may be tempting for each discipline involved in collaborative research to keep their own disciplinary purity—to publish in their discipline's journals and speak to their discipline's unique concerns and theory while operating as part of the collective project. It is far riskier for researchers to venture into each other's disciplinary territory. How can research claim to be interdisciplinary if no one takes this risk, though?

Just as computer scientists today seek to quantify culture, humanists are increasingly looking at ways to qualify computation. A comparison of the interdisciplinary research of two art historians—James Elkins and George Kubler—provides an example of two ways to approach scientific work as an art historian. Elkins, on one hand, seeks to maintain the purity of the outside discipline, taking care not to import "foreign" concepts. Kubler, on the other hand, embraced one of the most useful yet controversial tools in the humanist arsenal: metaphor.

James Elkins has investigated the image-making practices of researchers from a wide range of academic disciplines, profiling the differences in how humanists and scientists use images and visualizations in their work.[14] His research complicates the claims that art history and visual studies have on the study of images through in-depth discussion of the visualizations created and used in other disciplines, notably those in the natural sciences. Elkins's methodological stance is that these images should be discussed in a "noncausal" way.[15] In other words, he argues that commonly used visual studies methods that couch scientific illustration in terms of critical theory or historical context largely ignore the native languages of scientific disciplines and therefore ignore readers outside of the humanities.[16] Instead, he sets out to analyze these images in such a way as to appeal more or less equally to both humanities and natural science audiences, and he claims that he can build these cross-disciplinary bridges by avoiding metaphors "not found in the primary texts."[17] He writes, "It is crucial, I think to resist the desire to create continuous narratives out of specific practices, to decline the temptation to soften jargon, to refuse—at least temporarily—to assign meaning to apparently inarticulate computational practices."[18] This stance—and the struggle that he describes in avoiding interpretation, overarching frameworks, or metaphors for his writing—suggests that Elkins is aiming for a positivist ideal that he finds lacking in contemporary visual studies. This implies that the given "non-causal" method is virtuous insofar as it avoids "foreign metaphors."[19]

On the other hand, George Kubler, an art historian who challenged dominant art historical methods and theories of style with his influential book *The Shape of Time* (1962), employed metaphor liberally in his work. According to Reva Wolf, Kubler's use of metaphor was not only a "tool" that he used to understand historical processes but was central to his art-historical epistemology.[20] Wolf argues that metaphor is not incidental to Kubler's writing, but rather the methodology itself—a "methodology of metaphor." This is partly due to the emphasis that Kubler places on comparison in the history of art, but it goes much further than this. Metaphor brings together "one realm of experience with another."[21] For Kubler, metaphor was absolutely fundamental to the construction of his arguments. More specifically, metaphor was the means by which he could communicate his thoughts on pre-Columbian art to colleagues saturated by Western bias in art history. Metaphor is not a simple translation or a whimsical insertion of "foreign" terms into a separate discipline; it is a concrete means by which knowledge can be created. It opens new doors and pathways in our field of understanding.

Although Elkins argues at length that those in the natural sciences misunderstand or misuse philosophical/art historical terms like "beauty," he also appears to make his own assumptions about the nature of scientific imagery. At the outset of his research for an exhibition of images "across the university," he seems to proceed from the assumption that visualizations and images in the natural sciences are "useful" and yield direct scientific findings through their visual manifestation—another implied positivist virtue that would set scientific imagery apart from fine art. After discussing the images he collected with the researchers who created them, Elkins seems surprised to find that these researchers very often "abuse the visual" by creating "useless" images that do not actually aid in the effort to discover, measure, or quantify their research findings. Instead, the images are employed primarily for the (it is implied, degraded) purpose of publicity, to attract interest in the research from funders, administrators, and journals.[22] Elkins takes his positivist methods a step further still in attempting to create an encompassing taxonomy of the diverse image-making practices he describes, despite his repeated assertions that the images should not be polluted by interpretation outside the confines of their specific milieu.[23]

But why are researchers so afraid of this kind of methodological and interpretative pollution? The goal of interdisciplinary collaboration is to conduct research that benefits from differences in expertise. Bringing in untrained and unschooled members of one discipline to try to mimic the methods of a discipline outside of their own does not serve this purpose. Neither does applying one discipline's method to another's subject matter without acknowledging or learning from previous or existing research on that subject. More often than not, this is what leads to misunderstandings and recrimination between experts in different fields, who feel that someone unqualified is encroaching on their territory. An answer—if not a solution—to this is that researchers of different fields must "pollute" their subject matter in tandem. Interdisciplinary research may, therefore, harness the tool of metaphor as a way to reach across the epistemological divide. Perhaps such a tool can open up new pathways not only to understanding a particular subject but also to cultivating broader understanding across disciplines. Metaphor is a bridge that facilitates useful impurity in achieving collaborative goals.

Drawing from the analysis of machine learning in art history described in this book, one might begin to reimagine "digital" art history outside of the technology-specific paradigm in which it has been placed. What if it included the type of criticality toward new technology that disciplines like media studies have long employed without shying away from the "hard" science? What if interdisciplinary or transdisciplinary were multidirectional rather than the subsummation of the topics of one discipline within the methods of another? Metaphor is a powerful tool—not only for understanding the world around us but also for translating one paradigm of understanding into another. To assume that it is a mistake or an "abuse of science" is to miss the opportunity to foster a deeper level of interdisciplinary collaboration.[24] Achieving the goals of such collaborations does not mean taking turns dabbling in another field. Instead, researchers must harness the tools available to them in order to open *simultaneous* lines of communication between disciplines, built on mutual open-mindedness.

Appendix

Classification by Artistic Style, Publications in Computer Science, 2005–2021, Including the Development and Utilization of Fine Art Datasets

Dataset/Article	Subject/Source	Style Classifications
ArtHistorian[1] (2005) "Content-Based Access to Art Paintings"	Western painting Source: Internet (Web Museum Paris http://www.ibiblio.org/wm/)	Classicism, Cubism, Expressionism, Impressionism, Surrealism
Zujovic et al.[2] (2009) "Classifying Paintings by Artistic Genre: An Analysis of Features & Classifiers"	Western painting Source: Internet (unspecified)	Abstract Expressionism, Cubism, Impressionism, Pop Art, Realism
Siddiquie et al.[3] (2009) "Combining Multiple Kernels for Efficient Image Classification"	Western painting Source: Internet (unspecified)	Abstract Expressionist, Baroque, Cubism, Graffiti, Impressionist, Renaissance
Shamir et al.[4] (2010) "Impressionism, Expressionism, Surrealism: Automated Recognition of Painters and Schools of Art"	Modern Western painting Source: Internet (unspecified)	Abstract Expressionism, Impressionism, Surrealism
Čuljak et al.[5] (2011) "Classification of Art Paintings by Genre"	Western painting Source: "Google search engine" (i.e., internet)	Cubism, Fauvism, Impressionism, Naïve Art, Pointillism, Realism
Karayev et al.[6] (2013) "Recognizing Image Style"	Western painting + Ukiyo-e Source: Wikipaintings	Abstract Art, Abstract Expressionism, Art Informel, Art Nouveau (Modern), Baroque, Color Field Painting, Cubism, Early Renaissance, Expressionism, High Renaissance, Impressionism, Magic Realism, Mannerism (Late Renaissance), Minimalism, Naïve Art (Primitivism), Neoclassical, Northern Renaissance, Pop Art, Post-Impressionism, Realism, Rococo, Romanticism, Surrealism, Symbolism, Ukiyo-e

(continued)

Dataset/Article	Subject/Source	Style Classifications
Painting-91[7] (2014) "Painting-91: A Large Scale Database for Computational Painting Categorization"	Western painting Source: Internet (unspecified)	Abstract Expressionism, Baroque, Constructivism, Cubism, Impressionism, Neo-Classical, Pop Art, Postimpressionism, Realism, Renaissance, Romanticism, Surrealism, Symbolism
Saleh and Elgammal[8] (2015, 2016) "Large-Scale Classification of Fine-Art Paintings: Learning the Right Metric on the Right Feature"	Western painting + Ukiyo-e Source: WikiArt	**27 style categories:** Abstract Expressionism, Action Painting, Analytical Cubism, Art Nouveau–Modern Art, Baroque, Color Field Painting, Contemporary Realism, Cubism, Early Renaissance, Expressionism, Fauvism, High Renaissance, Impressionism, Mannerism-Late-Renaissance, Minimalism, New Realism, Northern Renaissance, Pointillism, Pop Art, Post Impressionism, Primitivism–Naive Art, Realism, Rococo, Romanticism, Symbolism, Synthetic Cubism, Ukiyo-e
Bar et al.[9] (2015) "Classification of Artistic Styles Using Binarized Features Derived from a Deep Neural Network"	Western painting + Ukiyo-e Source: WikiArt	(Same as above—27 WikiArt style categories)
Tan et al.[10] (2016) "Ceci n'est pas une pipe: A Deep Convolutional Network for Fine-Art Paintings Classification"	Western painting + Ukiyo-e Source: WikiArt	(Same as above—27 WikiArt style categories)
DeepArt[11] (2017) "DeepArt: Learning Joint Representations of Visual Arts"	"Everything" (primarily Western art) Sources: over 500,000 works from WikiArt, Web Gallery of Art, Rijksmuseum, Google Arts & Culture, images collected via Google (internet)	—
Elgammal et al.[12] (2018) "The Shape of Art History in the Eyes of the Machine"	Western painting + Ukiyo-e Source: WikiArt	**20 (amended categories):** Abstract-Expressionism, Art Nouveau, Baroque, Color field painting, Cubism, Early Renaissance, Expressionism, Fauvism, High Renaissance, Impressionism, Mannerism and Late Renaissance, Minimalism, Naïve art–Primitivism, Northern Renaissance, Pop-art, Post-Impressionism, Realism, Rococo, Romanticism, Ukiyo-e

Dataset/Article	Subject/Source	Style Classifications
SemArt[13] (2018) "How to Read Paintings: Semantic Art Understanding with Multi-Modal Retrieval"	Creation of SemArt: A collection of art images with textual attributes	—
OmniArt[14] (2018) "OmniArt: A Large-Scale Artistic Benchmark"	"Everything" (primarily Western art) Sources: over 2 million works from WikiArt, 16 museum collections (updating/scraping new content from these databases)	—
Gultepe et al.[15] (2018) "Predicting and Grouping Digitized Paintings by Style Using Unsupervised Feature Learning"	Western painting Source: abcartgallery (now "Olga's Gallery" https://www.freeart.com/gallery/)	Art Nouveau, Baroque, Expressionism, Impressionism, Post-Impressionism, Realism, Renaissance, Romanticism
Cetinic et al.[16] (2019) "A Deep Learning Perspective on Beauty, Sentiment, and Remembrance of Art"	Western painting + Ukiyo-e Source: Wikiart	Abstract Art, Abstract Expressionism, Academicism, Art Informel, Art Nouveau, Baroque, Color Field Painting, Cubism, Expressionism, Impressionism, Lyrical Abstraction, Magic Realism, Mannerism, Minimalism, Naïve art, Neoclassicism, Pop Art, Post-Impressionism, Realism, Renaissance, Rococo, Romanticism, Surrealism, Symbolism, Ukiyo-e
Sandoval et al.[17] (2019) "Two-Stage Deep Learning Approach to the Classification of Fine-Art Paintings"	Western painting + Ukiyo-e, + Australian Aboriginal Source: Wikiart (Wikiart-derived subset Pandora18K[18]), author-created Aboriginal category	*Dataset 1:* Australian Aboriginal Art, Expressionism, Impressionism, Post Impressionism, Realism, Romanticism *Dataset 2:* Abstract Expressionism, Art Nouveau (Modern), Australian Aboriginal Art, Baroque, Color Field Painting, Cubism, Early Renaissance, Expressionism, Fauvism, High Renaissance, Impressionism, Mannerism (Late Renaissance), Minimalism, Naïve Art (Primitivism), Northern Renaissance, Pop Art, Post Impressionism, Realism, Rococo, Romanticism, Symbolism, Ukiyo-e

(continued)

Dataset/Article	Subject/Source	Style Classifications
		Dataset 3: Abstract Art, Australian Aboriginal Art, Baroque, Byzantine Iconography, Cubism, Early Renaissance, Expressionism, Fauvism, High Renaissance, Impressionism, Naïve Art, Northern Renaissance, Pop Art, Post Impressionism, Realism, Rococo, Romanticism, Surrealism, Symbolism
Chen and Yang[19] (2019) "Recognizing the Style of Visual Arts via Adaptive Cross-Layer Correlation"	Painting-91 (see above)	Painting-91 styles (see above)
Gao et al.[20] (2020) "The Performance of Two CNN Methods in Artworks Aesthetic Feature Recognition"	Western art: 5 artists Source: "Best Artworks of All Time: Collection of Paintings of the 50 Most Influential Artists of All Time" (https://www.kaggle.com/ikarus777/best-artworks-of-all-time)	—
Zhong et al.[21] (2020) "Fine-Art Painting Classification via Two-Channel Dual Path Networks"	Western art + Ukiyo-e Source: WikiArt, Gallerix	Abstract Art, Abstract Expressionism, Art Informel, Art Nouveau (Modern), Baroque, Color Field painting, Conceptual Art, Cubism, Early Renaissance, Expressionism, High Renaissance, Impressionism, Mannerism (Late Renaissance), Minimalism, Naïve art (Primitivism), Neoclassical, Northern Renaissance, Pop Art, Post-Impressionism, Realism, Romanticism, Rococo, Surrealism, Symbolism, Ukiyo-e
Vaigh et al. (2021)[22] "GCNBoost: Artwork Classification by Label Propagation through a Knowledge Graph"	SemArt dataset[23] and Buddha statue[24] dataset	SemArt: "School" meaning nationality, "genre" including portrait, landscape, etc. Buddha statues style periods: China, Heian period, Kamakura period, and Nara period
Castellano et al.[25] (2021) "Integrating Contextual Knowledge to Visual Features for Fine Art Classification"	ArtGraph: an artistic knowledge graph based on WikiArt and DBpedia	—

Dataset/Article	Subject/Source	Style Classifications
Castellano and Vessio[26] (2021) "Deep Learning Approaches to Pattern Extraction and Recognition in Paintings and Drawings: An Overview"	This is a survey of deep learning and art analysis	—
Zhao et al.[27] (2021) "How to Represent Paintings: A Painting Classification Using Artistic Comments"	Western art Sources: Painting-91; WikiArt	See WikiArt style categories above
Zhao et al.[28] (2021) "Compare the Performance of the Models in Art Classification"	MultitaskPainting100K dataset (created by the authors)	—

Notes

Introduction

1. Brad Stone, "Google Figures Out How to Make People Care about Art: Selfies," Bloomberg, January 22, 2018, https://www.bloomberg.com/news/articles/2018-01-22/google-figures-out-how-to-make-people-care-about-art-selfies.

2. Rob Thubron, "Google App That Matches Selfies to Famous Paintings Tops the App Stores," TechSpot, January 17, 2018, https://www.techspot.com/news/72790-google-app-matches-selfies-famous-paintings-tops-app.html.

3. In this book, I have consciously adopted the use the gender-neutral pronouns they/their for singular hypothetical subjects.

4. "Art Selfie," Google Arts & Culture, accessed February 2, 2022, https://artsandculture.google.com/camera/selfie.

5. Hamza Shaban, "A Google App That Matches Your Face to Artwork Is Wildly Popular. It's Also Raising Privacy Concerns.," *Washington Post*, January 17, 2018, https://www.washingtonpost.com/news/the-switch/wp/2018/01/16/google-app-that-matches-your-face-to-artwork-is-wildly-popular-its-also-raising-privacy-concerns/; Arwa Mahdawi, "Finding Your Museum Doppelganger Is Fun—but the Science behind It Is Scary," *Guardian*, January 16, 2018, http://www.theguardian.com/commentisfree/2018/jan/16/find-your-art-doppelganger-facial-recognition-technology-frightening.

6. Stephen Pritchard, "The Artwashing of Gentrification and Social Cleansing," in *The Handbook of Displacement*, ed. Peter Adey et al. (Cham, Switzerland: Springer, 2020), 179–198.

7. Safiya Umoja Noble, *Algorithms of Oppression: How Search Engines Reinforce Racism* (New York: New York University Press, 2018); Meredith Broussard, *Artificial Unintelligence: How Computers Misunderstand the World* (Cambridge, MA: MIT Press, 2018); Virginia Eubanks, *Automating Inequality: How High Tech Tools Profile, Police, and Punish the Poor* (New York: Picador, 2018); Catherine D'Ignazio and Lauren F. Klein, *Data Feminism*

(Cambridge, MA: MIT Press, 2020); Caroline Criado-Perez, *Invisible Women: Exposing Data Bias in a World Designed for Men* (London: Vintage, 2020); Ruha Benjamin, *Race after Technology: Abolitionist Tools for the New Jim Code* (Cambridge: Polity, 2019).

8. More precisely, techniques for extracting the listed features include, among others, LBP (local binary patterns), GIST, HOG (histogram of orientation gradients), PHOG (pyramid of histogram of orientation gradients), and scale/transformation techniques such as SIFT, SURF, ORB, and BRIEF.

9. D. G. Lowe, "Object Recognition from Local Scale-Invariant Features," in *Proceedings of the Seventh IEEE International Conference on Computer Vision*, vol. 2, 1999, 1150–1157, https://doi.org/10.1109/ICCV.1999.790410.

10. For examples of artist and style classification research using SIFT, see Sergey Karayev et al., "Recognizing Image Style," arXiv:1311.3715 [cs.CV], November 15, 2013, https://doi.org/10.48550/arXiv.1311.3715; Fahad Shahbaz Khan et al., "Painting-91: A Large Scale Database for Computational Painting Categorization," *Machine Vision and Applications* 25, no. 6 (August 1, 2014): 1385–1397; Siddharth Agarwal et al., "Genre and Style Based Painting Classification," in *2015 IEEE Winter Conference on Applications of Computer Vision* (New York: IEEE, 2015), 588–594, https://doi.org/10.1109/WACV.2015.84.

11. Aude Oliva and Antonio Torralba, "Modeling the Shape of the Scene: A Holistic Representation of the Spatial Envelope," *International Journal of Computer Vision* 42, no. 3 (May 1, 2001): 145–175.

12. Karayev et al., "Recognizing Image Style."

13. T. Ojala, M. Pietikainen, and T. Maenpaa, "Multiresolution Gray-Scale and Rotation Invariant Texture Classification with Local Binary Patterns," *IEEE Transactions on Pattern Analysis and Machine Intelligence* 24, no. 7 (July 2002): 971–987.

14. Ojala, Pietikainen, and Maenpaa, 1.

15. Robert K. McConnell, Method of and apparatus for pattern recognition, US patent US4567610A, filed July 22, 1982, and issued January 28, 1986, https://patents.google.com/patent/US4567610/en; N. Dalal and B. Triggs, "Histograms of Oriented Gradients for Human Detection," in *2005 IEEE Computer Society Conference on Computer Vision and Pattern Recognition (CVPR'05)*, vol. 1 (New York: IEEE, 2005), 886–893, https://doi.org/10.1109/CVPR.2005.177.

16. For a survey of art categorization using deep learning, see Giovanna Castellano and Gennaro Vessio, "Deep Learning Approaches to Pattern Extraction and Recognition in Paintings and Drawings: An Overview," *Neural Computing and Applications* 33, no. 19 (October 1, 2021): 12263–12282. See also Wei Ren Tan et al., "Ceci n'est pas une pipe: A Deep Convolutional Network for Fine-Art Paintings Classification," in *2016 IEEE International Conference on Image Processing (ICIP)* (New York: IEEE, 2016), 3703–3707, https://doi.org/10.1109/ICIP.2016.7533051; Hui Mao, Ming Cheung,

and James She, "DeepArt: Learning Joint Representations of Visual Arts," in *Proceedings of the 25th ACM International Conference on Multimedia* (New York: ACM, 2017), 1183–1191, https://doi.org/10.1145/3123266.3123405.

17. Mao, Cheung, and She, "DeepArt," 3.

18. Dave Gershgorn, "The Inside Story of How AI Got Good Enough to Dominate Silicon Valley," Quartz, June 18, 2018, https://qz.com/1307091/the-inside-story-of-how-ai-got-good-enough-to-dominate-silicon-valley/; Alex Krizhevsky, Ilya Sutskever, and Geoffrey E. Hinton, "ImageNet Classification with Deep Convolutional Neural Networks," *Communications of the ACM* 60, no. 6 (May 24, 2017): 84–90.

19. This is noted by Anne Helmreich, citing Raymond Williams. Anne Helmreich et al., "Theses on Social Art History in the Age of Computational Methods," Humanities Commons, December 2021, 5, https://hcommons.org/deposits/item/hc:43511/.

20. Helmreich et al.

21. Jean-Baptiste Michel et al., "Quantitative Analysis of Culture Using Millions of Digitized Books," *Science* 331, no. 6014 (January 14, 2011): 176–182.

22. https://books.google.com/ngrams.

23. Michel et al., "Quantitative Analysis of Culture," 176.

24. Michel et al., 181.

25. Timothy Brennan, "The Digital-Humanities Bust," *Chronicle of Higher Education,* October 15, 2017, https://www.chronicle.com/article/The-Digital-Humanities-Bust/241424.

26. Geoffrey Nunberg, "Counting on Google Books," *Chronicle of Higher Education,* December 16, 2010, https://www.chronicle.com/article/Counting-on-Google-Books/125735; Patricia Cohen, "In 500 Billion Words, New Window on Culture," *New York Times,* December 16, 2010, https://www.nytimes.com/2010/12/17/books/17words.html; David Greetham, "The Resistance to Digital Humanities," in *Debates in the Digital Humanities,* ed. Matthew K. Gold (Minnesota: University of Minnesota Press, 2012), 448; Ted Underwood, "Dear Humanists: Fear Not the Digital Revolution," *Chronicle of Higher Education,* March 27, 2019, https://www.chronicle.com/article/Dear-Humanists-Fear-Not-the/245987.

27. Greetham, "The Resistance to Digital Humanities"; Stanley E. Fish, "What Is Stylistics and Why Are They Saying Such Terrible Things about It?," in *Approaches to Poetics,* ed. Seymour Chatman (New York: Chatman, 1973), 109–152.

28. Daniel Allington, Sarah Brouillette, and David Golumbia, "Neoliberal Tools (and Archives): A Political History of Digital Humanities," *Los Angeles Review of Books,* May 1, 2016, https://lareviewofbooks.org/article/neoliberal-tools-archives-political-history-digital-humanities/; Claire Bishop, "Against Digital Art History," *International Journal for Digital Art History,* no. 3 (July 27, 2018): 122–131.

29. Jonathan Kramnick, "The Interdisciplinary Delusion: Saving Disciplines Is the Only Way to Save Ourselves," *Chronicle of Higher Education*, October 11, 2018, https://www.chronicle.com/article/the-interdisciplinary-delusion/.

30. Geoffrey Rockwell and Stéfan Sinclair, *Hermeneutica: Computer-Assisted Interpretation in the Humanities* (Cambridge, MA: MIT Press, 2016), 21.

31. Paul R Gross and Norman Levitt, *Higher Superstition* (Baltimore: Johns Hopkins University Press, 1994).

32. Andrew Ross, "Introduction," *Social Text*, no. 46/47 (1996): 6–7.

33. Alan D. Sokal, "Transgressing the Boundaries: Toward a Transformative Hermeneutics of Quantum Gravity," *Social Text*, no. 46/47 (1996): 217–252.

34. Alan D. Sokal, "A Physicist Experiments with Cultural Studies," *Lingua Franca* 6, no. 4 (1996): 62–64.

35. Bruce Robbins and Andrew Ross, "Mystery Science Theater," *Lingua Franca* 6, no. 5 (1996): 54–57.

36. The term was solidified by two special issues in *Visual Resources* on the topic of "digital art history" in 2013 and 2019, and the advent of the *International Journal of Digital Art History* in 2015. See Murtha Baca and Anne Helmreich, eds., "Digital Art History," special issue, *Visual Resources* 29, no. 1–2 (2013); Murtha Baca, Anne Helmreich, and Melissa Gill, "Digital Art History," *Visual Resources* 35, no. 1–2 (April 3, 2019): 1–5.

37. For this, see Kathryn Brown, ed., *The Routledge Companion to Digital Humanities and Art History* (New York: Routledge, 2020).

38. One example of a group of researchers that included both computer vision researchers and art historians is the PRINTART group (http://printart.isr.ist.utl.pt/members.html). Tellingly, however, none of the art historians listed as group members serve as coauthors on the computer vision papers published by the group.

39. Susan Schreibman, Raymond George Siemens, and John Unsworth, eds., *A Companion to Digital Humanities* (Malden, MA: Blackwell, 2004); Benjamin Zweig, "Forgotten Genealogies: Brief Reflections on the History of Digital Art History," *International Journal for Digital Art History*, no. 1 (June 26, 2015): 38–49; Anna Bentkowska-Kafel, "Debating Digital Art History," *International Journal for Digital Art History*, no. 1 (June 26, 2015): 50–64.

40. Johanna Drucker, "Is There a 'Digital' Art History?," *Visual Resources* 29, no. 1–2 (June 1, 2013): 7.

41. Kathleen Fitzpatrick, "The Humanities, Done Digitally," *Chronicle of Higher Education*, May 8, 2011, https://www.chronicle.com/article/the-humanities-done-digitally/.

42. Park Doing and C. Richard Johnson Jr., "On Applying Signal Processing to Computational Art History: An Interview," *International Journal for Digital Art History*, no. 1 (June 26, 2015): 94.

43. Sarah Allison et al., "Quantitative Formalism: An Experiment," *N+1*, November 13, 2012, 81–108.

44. Pamela Fletcher and Anne Helmreich, "Digital Methods and the Study of the Art Market," in *The Routledge Companion to Digital Humanities and Art History*, edited by Kathryn Brown (New York: Routledge, 2020), 167–177; Pamela Fletcher et al., "Local/Global: Mapping Nineteenth-Century London's Art Market," *Nineteenth-Century Art Worldwide* 11, no. 3 (2012): 1–40; Anne Helmreich, Tim Hitchcock, and William J. Turkel, "Rethinking Inventories in the Digital Age: The Case of the Old Bailey," *Journal of Art Historiography*, no. 11 (2014): 1–25.

45. Noa Garcia and George Vogiatzis, "How to Read Paintings: Semantic Art Understanding with Multi-Modal Retrieval," arXiv:1810.09617 [cs.CV], October 22, 2018, http://arxiv.org/abs/1810.09617; Noa Garcia, Benjamin Renoust, and Yuta Nakashima, "ContextNet: Representation and Exploration for Painting Classification and Retrieval in Context," *International Journal of Multimedia Information Retrieval* 9, no. 1 (March 1, 2020): 17–30; Noa Garcia et al., "A Dataset and Baselines for Visual Question Answering on Art," arXiv:2008.12520 [cs.CV], August 28, 2020, http://arxiv.org/abs/2008.12520.

46. Giovanna Castellano, Giovanni Sansaro, and Gennaro Vessio, "Integrating Contextual Knowledge to Visual Features for Fine Art Classification," arXiv:2105.15028 [cs.CV], September 28, 2021, http://arxiv.org/abs/2105.15028.

47. Sofian Audry makes a similar point regarding art created by AI systems, arguing that the computer science aim to optimize can be at odds with artistic creation. See *Art in the Age of Machine Learning* (Cambridge, MA: MIT Press, 2021), 21–26.

48. Babak Saleh et al., "Toward Automated Discovery of Artistic Influence," *Multimedia Tools and Applications* 75, no. 7 (April 1, 2016): 3565–3591.

49. "Digital Humanities Laboratory at Rutgers," accessed October 14, 2019, https://sites.google.com/site/digihumanlab/home.

50. Anna Näslund Dahlgren and Amanda Wasielewski, "The Digital U-Turn in Art History," *Konsthistorisk Tidskrift/Journal of Art History* 90, no. 4 (December 13, 2021): 249–266.

51. A. M. Turing, "I.—Computing Machinery and Intelligence," *Mind* 59, no. 236 (October 1, 1950): 433–460, https://doi.org/10.1093/mind/LIX.236.433.

52. Geoffrey Rockwell and Stéfan Sinclair, *Hermeneutica: Computer-Assisted Interpretation in the Humanities* (Cambridge, MA: MIT Press, 2016), 17.

53. Rockwell and Sinclair, 161.

54. J. A. Emmens and Gary Schwartz, "Erwin Panofsky as a Humanist," *Simiolus: Netherlands Quarterly for the History of Art* 2, no. 3 (1967): 109–113; Erwin Panofsky, "The History of Art as a Humanistic Discipline," in *Meaning in the Visual Arts* (Garden City, NY: Doubleday Anchor, 1955), 1–25.

55. Johanna Drucker, "Humanities Approaches to Graphical Display," *Digital Humanities Quarterly* 5, no. 1 (March 10, 2011): 3, http://www.digitalhumanities.org/dhq/vol/5/1/000091/000091.html.

56. Drucker, 6.

57. Lev Manovich, "Museum without Walls, Art History without Names," in *The Oxford Handbook of Sound and Image in Digital Media*, ed. Carol Vernallis, Amy Herzog, and John Richardson (Oxford: Oxford University Press, 2013), 15; Lev Manovich, "Data Science and Digital Art History," *International Journal for Digital Art History*, no. 1 (2015): 17–18.

58. Lev Manovich, "Cultural Analytics: Visualizing Cultural Patterns in the Era of 'More Media,'" January 2009, http://manovich.net/index.php/projects/cultural-analytics-visualizing-cultural-patterns; Lev Manovich, *Cultural Analytics* (Cambridge, MA: MIT Press, 2020), 187–244.

59. Manovich, *Cultural Analytics*, 17.

60. Lev Manovich, "The Science of Culture? Social Computing, Digital Humanities and Cultural Analytics," *Journal of Cultural Analytics*, May 23, 2016, https://culturalanalytics.org/article/11060; Lev Manovich, "How to Follow Global Digital Cultures, or Cultural Analytics for Beginners," in *Deep Search: The Politics of Search beyond Google*, ed. Konrad Becker and Felix Stalder (Innsbruck, Austria: Studien Verlag, 2009), 204–205.

61. Lev Manovich, "Can We Think without Categories?," *Digital Culture & Society* 4, no. 1 (2018): 17–28.

62. Lev Manovich, "Data Science and Digital Art History," *International Journal for Digital Art History*, no. 1 (June 26, 2015): 24.

63. Franco Moretti, *Distant Reading* (London: Verso, 2013).

64. Moretti, 46.

65. Manovich, "Data Science and Digital Art History," 18.

66. Manovich, *Cultural Analytics*, 17.

67. Manovich, 17.

68. Andrew G. Ferguson, *The Rise of Big Data Policing: Surveillance, Race, and the Future of Law Enforcement* (New York: New York University Press, 2017), 123.

69. Lisa Gitelman and Virginia Jackson, "Introduction," in *"Raw Data" Is an Oxymoron*, ed. Lisa Gitelman (Cambridge, MA: MIT Press, 2013), 6.

70. "Not only do images make the atlas; atlas images make the science." Lorraine Daston and Peter Galison, *Objectivity* (New York: Zone Books, 2007), 22.

71. For further critical analysis of visualizations, see Johanna Drucker, *Visualization and Interpretation: Humanistic Approaches to Display* (Cambridge, MA: MIT Press, 2020).

72. Daston and Galison, *Objectivity*, 121.

73. Daston and Galison, 197–198, 262–263.

74. Daston and Galison, 372–374.

75. Daston and Galison, 10.

76. Daston and Galison, 376.

77. Daston and Galison, 376.

78. Daston and Galison, 30–37, 206–207.

79. Daston and Galison, 37.

80. Daston and Galison, 253–254.

81. One can see the concurrent response to research in embodied perception and gestalt psychology in art-historical circles in the early twentieth century in the work of Hans Sedlmayr.

82. Harald Klinke, "Big Image Data within the Big Picture of Art History," *International Journal for Digital Art History*, no. 2 (October 18, 2016): 25.

83. Amanda Wasielewski, "Lurking within Reach: Stereoscopic Photomicrography in the 1860s," *History of Photography* 39, no. 1 (January 2, 2015): 67.

84. Erwin Panofsky, "The History of Art as a Humanistic Discipline," in *The Meaning of the Humanities: Five Essays*, ed. Theodore Meyer Greene (Port Washington, NY: Kennikat Press, 1969), 91–118.

85. Daston and Galison, *Objectivity*, 314.

86. Alois Riegl, *Stilfragen* (Berlin: G. Siemens, 1893); Heinrich Wölfflin, *Kunstgeschichtliche Grundbegriffe: Das Problem der Stilentwicklung in der neueren Kunst* (Munich: Bruckmann, 1915).

87. Daston and Galison, *Objectivity*, 328.

88. It is noteworthy that I was reminded of this citation in the context of an essay in the first issue of the *International Journal for Digital Art History*, which points to the resurrection of interest in figures like Panofsky in digital art history literature. I had last encountered this essay in my first semester as a doctoral student at the City University of New York Graduate Center taking the art history department's methods course. See Elli Doulkaridou, "Reframing Art History," *International Journal for Digital Art History*, no. 1 (June 26, 2015): 67–68.

89. Panofsky, "The History of Art as a Humanistic Discipline," 1969, 106.

90. Panofsky, 109.

91. Panofsky, 110.

92. Henri Focillon, *The Life of Forms in Art*, trans. Charles B. Hogan and George Kubler (New York: Zone Books, 1989).

93. In the early twentieth century, art historians were keen to avoid the pitfalls of describing art as a formula of historically determined variables. For example, Henri Focillon accused Meyer Schapiro of being a follower of Hippolyte Taine. Walter B. Cahn, "Schapiro and Focillon," *Gesta* 41, no. 2 (2002): 131; Christopher S. Wood, *A History of Art History* (Princeton, NJ: Princeton University Press, 2019), 339.

94. George Kubler, *The Shape of Time: Remarks on the History of Things* (New Haven, CT: Yale University Press, 2008).

95. Mieke Bal et al., "Art History and Its Theories," *The Art Bulletin* 78, no. 1 (1996): 9.

96. David Summers, "'Form,' Nineteenth-Century Metaphysics, and the Problem of Art Historical Description," *Critical Inquiry* 15, no. 2 (January 1989): 372–406.

97. David Summers, "The 'Visual Arts' and the Problem of Art Historical Description," *Art Journal* 42, no. 4 (December 1, 1982): 301–310; David Summers, *Real Spaces: World Art History and the Rise of Western Modernism* (London: Phaidon, 2003).

98. Bal et al., "Art History and Its Theories," 9.

99. Norman Bryson, ed., *Calligram: Essays in New Art History from France* (Cambridge: Cambridge University Press, 1988); Jonathan Harris, *The New Art History: A Critical Introduction* (London: Routledge, 2007), 1–6.

100. Meyer Schapiro, "Style," in *Anthropology Today: An Encyclopedic Inventory*, ed. A. L. Kroeber (Chicago: University of Chicago Press, 1953), 287; John Williams, "Meyer Schapiro in Silos: Pursuing an Iconography of Style," *The Art Bulletin* 85, no. 3 (September 1, 2003): 442–468.

101. W. Eugene Kleinbauer, *Modern Perspectives in Western Art History: An Anthology of 20th-Century Writings on the Visual Arts* (New York: Holt, Rinehart and Winston, 1971), 37.

102. Bal et al., "Art History and Its Theories," 9–12.

103. Dahlgren and Wasielewski, "The Digital U-Turn in Art History."

104. Allison et al., "Quantitative Formalism."

105. Allison et al., 89.

106. Allison et al., 90.

107. Fabian Offert and Peter Bell, "Perceptual Bias and Technical Metapictures: Critical Machine Vision as a Humanities Challenge," *AI & Society*, October 12, 2020.

108. Mitra Azar, Geoff Cox, and Leonardo Impett, "Introduction: Ways of Machine Seeing," *AI & Society* 36 (2021): 1093–1104.

109. See Whitney Davis's longer discussion of the distinctions between formalism, stylistic analysis, and iconography. Davis ultimately argues that formalism cannot be separated from style or iconography, writing, "it is not at all clear that there really *are* any formal aspects of artworks (or any other kinds of objects) that can somehow be identified apart from or outside of stylistic and iconographic successions." Whitney Davis, *A General Theory of Visual Culture* (Princeton, NJ: Princeton University Press, 2011), 48.

110. Richard Neer, "Connoisseurship and the Stakes of Style," *Critical Inquiry* 32, no. 1 (2005): 11; Davis, *A General Theory of Visual Culture*, 46.

111. Davis, *A General Theory of Visual Culture*, 46.

112. Richard Wollheim, "Pictorial Style: Two Views," in *The Concept of Style*, ed. Berel Lang (Ithaca, NY: Cornell University Press, 1987), 183.

Chapter 1

1. Loris Nanni and Stefano Ghidoni, "How Could a Subcellular Image, or a Painting by Van Gogh, Be Similar to a Great White Shark or to a Pizza?," *Pattern Recognition Letters* 85 (January 1, 2017): 1–7.

2. Often a portion of the test set, called a "validation set" or "cross-validation set," is included and is used to fine tune the model.

3. Fahad Shahbaz Khan et al., "Painting-91: A Large Scale Database for Computational Painting Categorization," *Machine Vision and Applications* 25, no. 6 (August 1, 2014): 91.

4. Ahmed Elgammal et al., "The Shape of Art History in the Eyes of the Machine," arXiv:1801.07729 [cs.AI], January 23, 2018, p. 5, http://arxiv.org/abs/1801.07729v2.

5. Wei Ren Tan et al., "ArtGAN: Artwork Synthesis with Conditional Categorical GANs," arXiv:1702.03410 [cs.CV], February 11, 2017, http://arxiv.org/abs/1702.03410v2.

6. Anthony Hamber, Jean Miles, and William Vaughan, eds., *Computers and the History of Art* (London: Mansell, 1989); Benjamin Zweig, "Forgotten Genealogies: Brief Reflections on the History of Digital Art History," *International Journal for Digital Art History*, no. 1 (June 26, 2015): 38–49.

7. https://www.artstor.org/collection/mellon-international-dunhuang-archive/.

8. Mike Ananny and Kate Crawford, "Seeing without Knowing: Limitations of the Transparency Ideal and Its Application to Algorithmic Accountability," *New Media & Society* 20, no. 3 (March 1, 2018): 973–989.

9. Anna Dahlgren and Karin Hansson, "What an Image Is: The Ontological Gap between Researchers and Information Specialists," *Art Documentation: Journal of the Art Libraries Society of North America* 40, no. 1 (March 1, 2021): 21–32.

10. Julia Corrin et al., "CAMPI: Computer-Aided Metadata Generation for Photo Archives Initiative" (Carnegie Mellon University Libraries, 2020), https://kilthub.cmu .edu/articles/preprint/CAMPI_Computer-Aided_Metadata_Generation_for_Photo _archives_Initiative/12791807; Rebecca Bakker et al., "AI for Archives: Using Facial Recognition to Enhance Metadata" (Florida International University, 2020), https:// digitalcommons.fiu.edu/glworks/93/; Oonagh Murphy and Elena Villaespesa, "AI: A Museum Planning Toolkit," Report (London: Goldsmiths, University of London, January 2020), https://themuseumsai.network/toolkit/.

11. Sudeepti Surapaneni, Sana Syed, and Logan Yoonhyuk Lee, "Exploring Themes and Bias in Art Using Machine Learning Image Analysis," in *2020 Systems and Information Engineering Design Symposium (SIEDS)*, 2020, 1–6, https://doi.org/10.1109/SIEDS 49339.2020.9106656.

12. Virginia Eubanks, *Automating Inequality: How High-Tech Tools Profile, Police, and Punish the Poor* (New York: Picador, 2018); Safiya Umoja Noble, *Algorithms of Oppression: How Search Engines Reinforce Racism* (New York: New York University Press, 2018); Sara Wachter-Boettcher, *Technically Wrong: Sexist Apps, Biased Algorithms, and Other Threats of Toxic Tech* (New York: W. W. Norton, 2018); Ruha Benjamin, *Race after Technology: Abolitionist Tools for the New Jim Code* (Cambridge: Polity, 2019).

13. Kate Crawford and Trevor Paglen, "Excavating AI: The Politics of Images in Machine Learning Training Sets," 2019, https://www.excavating.ai/.

14. https://www.mturk.com/.

15. Orit Gat, "How AI Selfie App ImageNet Roulette Took the Internet by Storm," *Frieze*, accessed July 22, 2020, https://frieze.com/article/how-ai-selfie-app-imagenet -roulette-took-internet-storm; Cade Metz, "'Nerd,' 'Nonsmoker,' 'Wrongdoer': How Might A.I. Label You?," *New York Times*, September 20, 2019, https://www.nytimes .com/2019/09/20/arts/design/imagenet-trevor-paglen-ai-facial-recognition.html.

16. Crawford and Paglen, "Excavating AI."

17. Adam Harvey and Jules LaPlace, MegaPixels, 2017–2020, https://exposing.ai/about/.

18. Svetlana Alpers, "Style Is What You Make It: The Visual Arts Once Again," in *The Concept of Style*, ed. Berel Lang (Ithaca, NY: Cornell University Press, 1987), 137.

19. Khan et al., "Painting-91," 1385.

20. C. Colombo, A. Del Bimbo, and P. Pala, "Semantics in Visual Information Retrieval," *IEEE MultiMedia* 6, no. 3 (July 1999): 38–53.

21. Colombo, Del Bimbo, and Pala, 38–39.

22. For a broader look at limitations see Anja Bechmann and Geoffrey C. Bowker, "Unsupervised by Any Other Name: Hidden Layers of Knowledge Production in Artificial Intelligence on Social Media," *Big Data & Society* 6, no. 1 (January 1, 2019): 1–11.

23. Lev Manovich, "Data Science and Digital Art History," *International Journal for Digital Art History*, no. 1 (2015): 12–35; Lev Manovich, "Cultural Analytics, Social Computing and Digital Humanities," in *The Datafied Society*, ed. Mirko Tobias Schäfer and Karin van Es (Amsterdam: Amsterdam University Press, 2017), 55–68; Lev Manovich, "Can We Think without Categories?," *Digital Culture & Society* 4, no. 1 (2018): 17–28.

24. Khan et al., "Painting-91," 1393.

25. Ying Liu et al., "A Survey of Content-Based Image Retrieval with High-Level Semantics," *Pattern Recognition* 40, no. 1 (January 1, 2007): 263.

26. Wei Ren Tan et al., "Ceci n'est pas une pipe: A Deep Convolutional Network for Fine-Art Paintings Classification," in *2016 IEEE International Conference on Image Processing (ICIP)* (New York: IEEE, 2016), 3703–3707, https://doi.org/10.1109/ICIP.2016.7533051.

27. Jana Zujovic et al., "Classifying Paintings by Artistic Genre: An Analysis of Features & Classifiers," in *2009 IEEE International Workshop on Multimedia Signal Processing* (New York: IEEE, 2009), 1, https://ieeexplore.ieee.org/document/5293271.

28. Michel Foucault, *This Is Not a Pipe*, trans. James Harkness (Berkeley: University of California Press, 1983).

29. Crawford and Paglen, "Excavating AI."

30. Catherine Sandoval, Elena Pirogova, and Margaret Lech, "Two-Stage Deep Learning Approach to the Classification of Fine-Art Paintings," *IEEE Access* 7 (2019): 41770–41781, https://doi.org/10.1109/ACCESS.2019.2907986.

31. B. Günsel, S. Sariel, and O. Icoglu, "Content-Based Access to Art Paintings," in *IEEE International Conference on Image Processing 2005*, vol. 2 (New York: IEEE, 2005), 558, doi: 10.1109/ICIP.2005.1530116.

32. Günsel, Sariel, and Icoglu, 1.

33. Günsel, Sariel, and Icoglu, 1, 3.

34. Zujovic et al., "Classifying Paintings by Artistic Genre," 1.

35. Gjorgji Strezoski and Marcel Worring, "OmniArt: A Large-Scale Artistic Benchmark," *ACM Transactions on Multimedia Computing, Communications, and Applications* 14, no. 4, article no. 88 (October 23, 2018): 2, https://doi.org/10.1145/3273022.

36. Behjat Siddiquie, Shiv N. Vitaladevuni, and Larry S. Davis, "Combining Multiple Kernels for Efficient Image Classification," in *2009 Workshop on Applications of*

Computer Vision (WACV) (New York: IEEE, 2009), 2, https://doi.org/10.1109/WACV.2009.5403040.

37. Nicolas Gonthier et al., "Weakly Supervised Object Detection in Artworks," in *Proceedings of the European Conference on Computer Vision (ECCV)* (Cham, Switzerland: Springer, 2018), 1, https://doi.org/10.48550/arXiv.1810.02569.

38. Sheng-hua Zhong, Xingsheng Huang, and Zhijiao Xiao, "Fine-Art Painting Classification via Two-Channel Dual Path Networks," *International Journal of Machine Learning and Cybernetics* 11, no. 1 (January 1, 2020): 137–152, https://doi.org/10.1007/s13042-019-00963-0.

39. Alpers, "Style Is What You Make It," 137.

40. Babak Saleh and Ahmed Elgammal, "Large-Scale Classification of Fine-Art Paintings: Learning the Right Metric on the Right Feature," arXiv:1505.00855 [cs.CV], May 5, 2015, 5, https://arxiv.org/abs/1505.00855.

41. Hui Mao, Ming Cheung, and James She, "DeepArt: Learning Joint Representations of Visual Arts," in *Proceedings of the 25th ACM International Conference on Multimedia* (New York: ACM, 2017), 1183–1191, https://doi.org/10.1145/3123266.3123405.

42. Meredith Broussard, *Artificial Unintelligence: How Computers Misunderstand the World* (Cambridge, MA: MIT Press, 2018), 33–37.

43. Khan et al., "Painting-91," 1387.

44. Harry Wechsler and Andeep S. Toor, "Modern Art Challenges Face Detection," *Pattern Recognition Letters* 126 (September 1, 2019): 3–10.

45. Wechsler and Toor, "Modern Art Challenges Face Detection," 3.

46. Robinson Meyer, "Anti-Surveillance Camouflage for Your Face," *The Atlantic*, July 24, 2014, https://www.theatlantic.com/technology/archive/2014/07/makeup/374929/.

47. Jia Li and J. Z. Wang, "Studying Digital Imagery of Ancient Paintings by Mixtures of Stochastic Models," *IEEE Transactions on Image Processing* 13, no. 3 (March 2004): 340.

48. Elgammal et al., "The Shape of Art History," 3.

49. Matthew L. Jockers, *Macroanalysis: Digital Methods and Literary History* (Urbana: University of Illinois Press, 2013); Andrew Piper, *Enumerations: Data and Literary Study* (Chicago: University of Chicago Press, 2018), xi; James E. Dobson, *Critical Digital Humanities: The Search for a Methodology* (Urbana: University of Illinois Press, 2019), 19.

50. Ted Underwood, *Distant Horizons: Digital Evidence and Literary Change* (Chicago: University of Chicago Press, 2019), ix.

51. Jockers, *Macroanalysis*, 7.

52. Nan Z. Da, "The Computational Case against Computational Literary Studies," *Critical Inquiry* 45, no. 3 (March 1, 2019): 601–639.

53. Lev Manovich, "How to Compare One Million Images?," in *Understanding Digital Humanities*, ed. David M. Berry (London: Palgrave Macmillan, 2012), 252.

54. Robert Jensen, "Measuring Canons: Reflections on Innovation and the Nineteenth-Century Canon of European Art," in *Partisan Canons*, ed. Anna Brzyski (Durham, NC: Duke University Press, 2007), 27–28.

55. Saleh and Elgammal, "Large-Scale Classification of Fine-Art Paintings" (2015).

56. Mao, Cheung, and She, "DeepArt"; Strezoski and Worring, "OmniArt."

57. Shuqiang Jiang et al., "An Effective Method to Detect and Categorize Digitized Traditional Chinese Paintings," *Pattern Recognition Letters* 27, no. 7 (May 1, 2006): 734–746; Zujovic et al., "Classifying Paintings by Artistic Genre."

58. Jiang et al.

59. Sergey Karayev et al., "Recognizing Image Style," arXiv:1311.3715 [cs.CV], November 15, 2013, https://doi.org/10.48550/arXiv.1311.3715.

60. Sandoval, Pirogova, and Lech, "Two-Stage Deep Learning Approach," 41774.

61. Sandoval, Pirogova, and Lech, 41779.

62. Saleh and Elgammal, "Large-Scale Classification of Fine-Art Paintings" (2015), 2–3.

63. Lior Shamir et al., "Impressionism, Expressionism, Surrealism: Automated Recognition of Painters and Schools of Art," *ACM Transactions on Applied Perception* 7, no. 2, article 8 (February 25, 2010): 3, https://doi.org/10.1145/1670671.1670672.

64. This has also long been an issue for manual cataloguing of digital collections. See L. Hollink et al., "Classification of User Image Descriptions," *International Journal of Human-Computer Studies* 61, no. 5 (November 1, 2004): 606, https://doi.org/10.1016/j.ijhcs.2004.03.002.

65. Lev Manovich, *Cultural Analytics* (Cambridge, MA: MIT Press, 2020), 169.

66. Manovich, 169–172.

67. Wechsler and Toor, "Modern Art Challenges Face Detection," 6.

68. A. Leykin, F. Cutzu, and R. Hammoud, "Visual Properties Differentiating Art from Real Scenes," *Technical Report No. 565* (2002).

69. Panos Achlioptas et al., "ArtEmis: Affective Language for Visual Art," arXiv: 2101.07396 [cs.CV], January 18, 2021, http://arxiv.org/abs/2101.07396; Aliide Naylor, "Underpaid Workers Are Being Forced to Train Biased AI on Mechanical Turk," *Motherboard* (blog), March 8, 2021, https://www.vice.com/en/article/88apnv/underpaid-workers-are-being-forced-to-train-biased-ai-on-mechanical-turk.

70. https://www.wikiart.org/en/about.

71. Partha Mitter, "Decentering Modernism: Art History and Avant-Garde Art from the Periphery," *The Art Bulletin* 90, no. 4 (2008): 531–548.

72. Karayev et al., "Recognizing Image Style"; Eva Cetinic, Tomislav Lipic, and Sonja Grgic, "A Deep Learning Perspective on Beauty, Sentiment, and Remembrance of Art," *IEEE Access* 7 (2019): 73694–73710, https://doi.org/10.1109/ACCESS.2019.2921101; Sandoval, Pirogova, and Lech, "Two-Stage Deep Learning Approach."

73. Siddiquie, Vitaladevuni, and Davis, "Combining Multiple Kernels for Efficient Image Classification."

74. Wechsler and Toor, "Modern Art Challenges Face Detection," 5–6.

75. E. H. Gombrich, *Art and Illusion: A Study in the Psychology of Pictorial Representation* (London: Phaidon, 1960); Suzi Gablik, *Progress in Art* (New York: Rizzoli, 1976).

76. Vilayanur S. Ramachandran and William Hirstein, "The Science of Art: A Neurological Theory of Aesthetic Experience," *Journal of Consciousness Studies* 6, no. 6–7 (1999): 15–51.

77. Khan et al., "Painting-91," 1385; Shamir et al., "Impressionism, Expressionism, Surrealism," 2.

78. Zujovic et al., "Classifying Paintings by Artistic Genre," 2.

79. Shamir et al., "Impressionism, Expressionism, Surrealism," 3.

80. Some would separate Pollock and Rothko as well but, generally speaking, they were both working in abstract styles in New York City at the same time. For this reason, their work has been grouped under the broad umbrella of Abstract Expressionism.

81. Joan M. Marter, *Abstract Expressionism: The International Context* (New Brunswick, NJ: Rutgers University Press, 2007), 16, 233n10.

82. Alpers, "Style Is What You Make It."

83. Richard Neer, "Connoisseurship and the Stakes of Style," *Critical Inquiry* 32, no. 1 (2005): 11n28.

84. Khan et al., "Painting-91," 1386.

85. Manovich, "How to Compare One Million Images?," 258.

86. Khan et al., "Painting-91," 1388.

87. Mao, Cheung, and She, "DeepArt," 2.

88. Eren Gultepe, Thomas Edward Conturo, and Masoud Makrehchi, "Predicting and Grouping Digitized Paintings by Style Using Unsupervised Feature Learning," *Journal of Cultural Heritage* 31 (May 1, 2018): 14.

89. Strezoski and Worring, "OmniArt," 14.

90. Strezoski and Worring, 18.

91. Cetinic, Lipic, and Grgic, "A Deep Learning Perspective."

92. Alpers, "Style Is What You Make It," 138.

93. Michael Shanks, *The Classical Archaeology of Greece: Experiences of the Discipline* (London: Taylor & Francis, 1996), 35.

94. Saleh and Elgammal, "Large-Scale Classification of Fine-Art Paintings" (2015), 13.

95. Saleh and Elgammal, 13–14.

96. Sandoval, Pirogova, and Lech, "Two-Stage Deep Learning Approach," 41780.

97. Meyer Schapiro, "Style," in *Anthropology Today: An Encyclopedic Inventory*, ed. A. L. Kroeber (Chicago: University of Chicago Press, 1953), 288.

98. Fred Orton, "Action, Revolution and Painting," *Oxford Art Journal* 14, no. 2 (1991): 16n53; Harold Rosenberg, "The American Action Painters," *Art News* 51, no. 8 (1952): 22–23, 48–50.

99. Orton, "Action, Revolution and Painting."

100. Rosenberg, "The American Action Painters," 23.

101. Robert Coates, "The Art Galleries: Abroad and at Home," *New Yorker* 12 (1946): 29; Helen A. Harrison, "Arthur G. Dove and the Origins of Abstract Expressionism," *American Art* 12, no. 1 (1998): 75–76.

102. Rosenberg, "The American Action Painters," 23.

103. Günsel, Sariel, and Icoglu, "Content-Based Access to Art Paintings," 1.

104. Walter B. Cahn, "Schapiro and Focillon," *Gesta* 41, no. 2 (2002): 129–136.

105. Crawford and Paglen, "Excavating AI."

106. Zujovic et al., "Classifying Paintings by Artistic Genre," 2–3.

107. Heinrich Wölfflin, *Principles of Art History: The Problem of the Development of Style in Later Art*, trans. M. D. Hottinger (New York: Dover, 1950), 9.

108. Elgammal et al., "The Shape of Art History," 2.

109. Elgammal et al., 3.

110. Saleh and Elgammal, "Large-Scale Classification of Fine-Art Paintings" (2015); Babak Saleh and Ahmed Elgammal, "Large-Scale Classification of Fine-Art Paintings: Learning the Right Metric on the Right Feature," *International Journal for Digital Art History*, no. 2 (October 18, 2016): 70–93.

111. Elgammal et al., "The Shape of Art History," 5–6.

112. Strezoski and Worring, "OmniArt," 15.

113. Mao, Cheung, and She, "DeepArt," 2.

114. Mateja Čuljak et al., "Classification of Art Paintings by Genre," in *2011 Proceedings of the 34th International Convention MIPRO* (New York: IEEE, 2011), 1636, https://ieeexplore.ieee.org/document/5967323.

115. Jensen, "Measuring Canons."

116. Jensen, 48.

117. Jensen, 34.

118. Jensen, 34–35.

119. Underwood, *Distant Horizons*.

120. Schapiro, "Style," 288.

121. Manovich, "Data Science and Digital Art History"; Lev Manovich, "Museum without Walls, Art History without Names," in *The Oxford Handbook of Sound and Image in Digital Media*, ed. Carol Vernallis, Amy Herzog, and John Richardson (Oxford: Oxford University Press, 2013), 253–278.

122. Manovich, "Can We Think without Categories?," 25–26.

123. Manovich, "How to Compare One Million Images?," 263.

124. "Note that our method does not imply that we are getting rid of discrete categories completely. Rather, instead of being limited to a few provided by language, we can now define as many as we need." Manovich, "How to Compare One Million Images?," 264.

125. Manovich, "Can We Think without Categories?," 25.

126. Manovich, 26.

127. Claire Bishop, "Against Digital Art History," *International Journal for Digital Art History*, no. 3 (July 27, 2018): 122–131.

128. Lev Manovich, "Aesthetics," in *Keywords for Media Studies*, ed. Laurie Ouellette and Jonathan Gray (New York: New York University Press, 2017), 11.

129. Manovich, "How to Compare One Million Images?," 253.

130. Manovich, 270.

131. Manovich, 274.

132. Surapaneni, Syed, and Lee, "Exploring Themes and Bias in Art," 1.

CHAPTER 2

1. The first art history survey texts, like the first public museums, were driven by a desire to formulate a national identity through art and culture. See Carol Duncan and Alan

Wallach, "The Universal Survey Museum," *Art History* 3, no. 4 (1980): 252–257; Mitchell Schwarzer, "Origins of the Art History Survey Text," *Art Journal* 54, no. 3 (1995): 24–29.

2. Bradford R. Collins, "Rethinking the Introductory Art History Survey: A Practical, Somewhat Theoretical, and Inspirational Guide," *Art Journal* 54, no. 3 (1995): 23; Mark Miller Graham, "The Future of Art History and the Undoing of the Survey," *Art Journal* 54, no. 3 (1995): 30–34; Josh Yavelberg, "Questioning the Survey: A Look into Art History Survey and Its Pedagogical Practices," *Journal of Mason Graduate Research* 1, no. 1 (January 28, 2014): 23–48; Melissa Kerin and Andrea Lepage, "De-Centering 'The' Survey: The Value of Multiple Introductory Surveys to Art History," *Art History Pedagogy & Practice* 1, no. 1 (December 16, 2016), https://academicworks.cuny.edu/ahpp/vol1/iss1/3; Julia Sienkewicz, "Against the 'Coverage' Mentality: Rethinking Learning Outcomes and the Core Curriculum," *Art History Pedagogy & Practice* 1, no. 1 (December 16, 2016), https://academicworks.cuny.edu/ahpp/vol1/iss1/5; Virginia Spivey, Andy Schulz, and James Hopfensperger, "Measuring College Learning in Art History" (New York: Social Science Research Council, 2018), http://highered.ssrc.org/projects/measuring-college-learning-project/.

3. According to Richard Neer, the definition of connoisseurship should not be confined to identification of individual authors. Neer writes, "the connoisseur who attributes a painting to Rembrandt is performing the same actions, and for the same reasons, as the field archaeologist who sorts her finds at the end of the day." See Richard Neer, "Connoisseurship and the Stakes of Style," *Critical Inquiry* 32, no. 1 (2005): 3.

4. Jaynie Anderson, "The Political Power of Connoisseurship in Nineteenth-Century Europe: Wilhelm von Bode versus Giovanni Morelli," *Jahrbuch Der Berliner Museen* 38 (1996): 107.

5. Giovanni Morelli, *Italian Painters: Critical Studies of Their Works*, trans. Constance Jocelyn Ffoulkes (London: John Murray, 1907), 84–86.

6. Helen Rees Leahy, "'For Connoisseurs': *The Burlington Magazine* 1903–11," in *Art History and Its Institutions: The Nineteenth Century*, ed. Elizabeth Mansfield (London: Routledge, 2002), 231–245.

7. Michael Shanks, *The Classical Archaeology of Greece: Experiences of the Discipline* (London: Taylor & Francis, 1996), 36; Carlo Ginzburg and Anna Davin, "Morelli, Freud and Sherlock Holmes: Clues and Scientific Method," *History Workshop*, no. 9 (1980): 5–36.

8. Neer, "Connoisseurship and the Stakes of Style," 3.

9. Svetlana Alpers, "Style Is What You Make It: The Visual Arts Once Again," in *The Concept of Style*, ed. Berel Lang (Ithaca, NY: Cornell University Press, 1987), 139.

10. Alison Langmead et al., "Leonardo, Morelli, and the Computational Mirror," *Digital Humanities Quarterly* 15, no. 1 (March 5, 2021): 16, http://www.digitalhumanities.org/dhq/vol/15/1/000540/000540.html.

11. Sarah Allison et al., "Quantitative Formalism: An Experiment," *N+1*, November 13, 2012, 107.

12. Walter Benjamin, "The Work of Art in the Age of Its Technological Reproducibility," in *The Work of Art in the Age of Its Technological Reproducibility, and Other Writings on Media*, ed. Michael William Jennings, Brigid Doherty, and Thomas Y. Levin, trans. Edmund Jephcott, Rodney Livingstone, and Howard Eiland (Cambridge, MA: Belknap Press of Harvard University Press, 2008), 19–55.

13. This is not without precedent. Photographic images were used as a tool by nineteenth-century connoisseurs. Berenson had an extensive photograph collection and was comfortable determining the authenticity of artworks on the basis of these photographs. See Giovanni Pagliarulo, "Photographs to Read: Berensonian Annotations," in *Photo Archives and the Photographic Memory of Art History*, ed. Constanza Caraffa (Berlin: Deutscher Kunstverlag, 2011), 181–191; Fiorella Gioffredi Superbi, "The Photograph and Bernard Berenson: The Story of a Collection," *Visual Resources* 26, no. 3 (September 1, 2010): 289–303.

14. Langmead et al. argue that questions of efficiency are ill-suited to the humanities. I would clarify that this pertains to humanities research questions but not to humanities disciplines more generally. Computational tools already have an effect on the so-called efficiency of humanities research with little harm done to the core concerns of these disciplines. Where issues arise, rather, is in the conflation of humanities and computer science *research* aims. The core aim of humanities research is, therefore, not in the service of devising "more efficient" methods per se. See Langmead et al., "Leonardo, Morelli, and the Computational Mirror," 24.

15. S. Zhang, Y. Wu, and J. Chang, "Survey of Image Recognition Algorithms," in *2020 IEEE 4th Information Technology, Networking, Electronic and Automation Control Conference (ITNEC)*, vol. 1 (New York: IEEE, 2020), 542–548, doi: 10.1109/ITNEC48623.2020.9084972.

16. Anna Dahlgren and Karin Hansson, "What an Image Is: The Ontological Gap between Researchers and Information Specialists," *Art Documentation: Journal of the Art Libraries Society of North America* 40, no. 1 (March 1, 2021): 21–32.

17. Gustavo Carneiro et al., "Artistic Image Classification: An Analysis on the Printart Database," in *Computer Vision—ECCV 2012*, ed. Andrea Fusiello, Vittorio Murino, and Rita Cucchiara (Cham, Switzerland: Springer, 2012), 143–157; Nicholas Westlake, Hongping Cai, and Peter Hall, "Detecting People in Artwork with CNNs," in *Computer Vision—ECCV 2016*, ed. Gang Hua and Hervé Jégou (Cham, Switzerland: Springer, 2016), 825–841; Elliot J. Crowley and Andrew Zisserman, "The Art of Detection," in Hua and Jégou, *Computer Vision—ECCV 2016*, 721–737; Naoto Inoue et al., "Cross-Domain Weakly-Supervised Object Detection through Progressive Domain Adaptation," in *Proceedings of the IEEE Conference on Computer Vision and Pattern Recognition* (New York: IEEE, 2018), 5001–5009; Nicolas Gonthier et al.,

"Weakly Supervised Object Detection in Artworks," in *Computer Vision—ECCV 2018*, ed. Vittorio Ferrari, Martial Hebert, Cristian Sminchisescu, and Yair Weiss (Cham, Switzerland: Springer, 2018), 1–18.

18. Erwin Panofsky, *Studies in Iconology: Humanistic Themes in the Art of the Renaissance* (New York: Harper & Row, 1972), 9.

19. Although automated metadata tagging is rising in prominence, it still requires initial training sets that are manually labeled. The interpretative labels have to come intially from humans. See Rebecca Bakker et al., "AI for Archives: Using Facial Recognition to Enhance Metadata" (Miami: Florida International University, 2020), https://digitalcommons.fiu.edu/glworks/93/; Julia Corrin et al., "CAMPI: Computer-Aided Metadata Generation for Photo Archives Initiative" (Pittsburgh: Carnegie Mellon University Libraries, 2020), https://kilthub.cmu.edu/articles/preprint/CAMPI_Computer-Aided_Metadata_Generation_for_Photo_archives_Initiative/12791807; Oonagh Murphy and Elena Villaespesa, *AI: A Museum Planning Toolkit* (London: Goldsmiths, University of London, January 2020), https://themuseumsai.network/toolkit/.

20. Elliot J. Crowley and Andrew Zisserman, "The State of the Art: Object Retrieval in Paintings Using Discriminative Regions," in *Proceedings of the British Machine Vision Conference*, ed. Michel Valstar, Andrew French and Tony Pridmore (Durham, UK: BMVA Press, 2014).

21. Crowley and Zisserman, 1.

22. Anna Näslund Dahlgren and Amanda Wasielewski, "The Digital U-Turn in Art History," *Journal of Art History (Konsthistorisk Tidskrift)* 90, no. 4 (2021), December 13, 2021): 249–266.

23. Ahmed Elgammal, Yan Kang, and Milko Den Leeuw, "Picasso, Matisse, or a Fake? Automated Analysis of Drawings at the Stroke Level for Attribution and Authentication," *Proceedings of the AAAI Conference on Artificial Intelligence* 32, no. 1 (April 25, 2018): 2, https://ojs.aaai.org/index.php/AAAI/article/view/11313.

24. Langmead et al., "Leonardo, Morelli, and the Computational Mirror."

25. Documentation, however, is not foolproof. Provenance forgeries are relatively common. See Neer, "Connoisseurship and the Stakes of Style," 4.

26. Ben Lewis, *The Last Leonardo* (London: William Collins, 2019), 19.

27. Jamie Doward, "The Mystery of the Missing Leonardo: Where Is Da Vinci's $450m Jesus?," *Guardian*, October 13, 2019, http://www.theguardian.com/artanddesign/2019/oct/13/leonardo-da-vinci-salvator-mundi-jesus-louvre-exhibition.

28. David D. Kirkpatrick and Elaine Sciolino, "A Clash of Wills Keeps a Leonardo Masterpiece Hidden," *New York Times*, April 11, 2021, https://www.nytimes.com/2021/04/11/arts/design/salvator-mundi-louvre-leonardo.html.

29. Gareth Harris, "Leonardo Da Vinci's Salvator Mundi—the World's Most Expensive Work of Art—to Be Turned into an NFT," *The Art Newspaper*, April 2, 2021, http://www.theartnewspaper.com/news/leonardo-da-vinci-s-salvator-mundi-turned-into-an-nft.

30. Alison Langmead et al., "Leonardo, Morelli, and the Computational Mirror," *Digital Humanities Quarterly* 15, no. 1 (March 5, 2021), 26, http://www.digitalhumanities.org/dhq/vol/15/1/000540/000540.html.

31. A relevant contemporary example of this can be found in the artistic copy industry of Dafen in China. See Winnie Won Yin Wong, *Van Gogh on Demand: China and the Readymade* (Chicago: University of Chicago Press, 2014).

32. Jonathan Harris, *The New Art History: A Critical Introduction* (London: Routledge, 2007), 14.

33. See, for art practice, the integration of film, video, and advertising (pop art) into "high art" practice in the 1960s and 1970s. See also cultural critiques including Clement Greenberg, "Avant-Garde and Kitsch," in *Art in Theory, 1900–2000: An Anthology of Changing Ideas*, ed. Charles Harrison (Malden, MA: Blackwell, 2003), 539–549; Theodor Adorno and Max Horkheimer, "The Culture Industry: Enlightenment as Mass Deception," in *The Cultural Studies Reader*, 2nd ed., ed. Simon During (London: Routledge, 1999), 31–41.

34. "Visual Culture Questionnaire," *October* 77 (1996): 25–70.

35. This is not a case of "mission accomplished," however. Debates on how to "decolonize" art history, museums, and artistic practice are currently ongoing. Huey Copeland et al., "A Questionnaire on Decolonization," *October* 174 (December 1, 2020): 3–125.

36. Lev Manovich, *Cultural Analytics* (Cambridge, MA: MIT Press, 2020), 149–150; Ted Underwood, *Distant Horizons: Digital Evidence and Literary Change* (Chicago: University of Chicago Press, 2019); Franco Moretti, *Distant Reading* (London: Verso, 2013).

37. Neer, "Connoisseurship and the Stakes of Style," 12.

38. Whitney Davis, *A General Theory of Visual Culture* (Princeton, NJ: Princeton University Press, 2011), 46; Neer, "Connoisseurship and the Stakes of Style," 11.

39. See Jehane Ragai, *The Scientist and the Forger: Insights into the Scientific Detection of Forgery in Paintings* (London: Imperial College Press, 2015).

40. Vanessa Buhrmester, David Münch, and Michael Arens, "Analysis of Explainers of Black Box Deep Neural Networks for Computer Vision: A Survey," arXiv:1911.12116 [cs.AI], November 27, 2019, 1, http://arxiv.org/abs/1911.12116.

41. Finale Doshi-Velez and Been Kim, "Towards a Rigorous Science of Interpretable Machine Learning," arXiv:1702.08608 [stat.ML], February 28, 2017, http://arxiv.org/abs/1702.08608v2; Ning Xie et al., "Explainable Deep Learning: A Field Guide for the Uninitiated," arXiv:2004.14545 [cs.LG], April 30, 2020, http://arxiv.org/abs/2004.14545v1.

42. Elizabeth A. Holm, "In Defense of the Black Box," *Science* 364, no. 6435 (April 5, 2019): 26.

43. For the early development of feature visualization, see Karen Simonyan, Andrea Vedaldi, and Andrew Zisserman, "Deep Inside Convolutional Networks: Visualising Image Classification Models and Saliency Maps," arXiv:1312.6034 [cs.CV], April 19, 2014, http://arxiv.org/abs/1312.6034.

44. For a survey covering a variety of such techniques, see Quan-shi Zhang and Song-chun Zhu, "Visual Interpretability for Deep Learning: A Survey," *Frontiers of Information Technology & Electronic Engineering* 19, no. 1 (January 1, 2018): 27–39, https://doi.org/10.1631/FITEE.1700808.

45. Nicolas Gonthier, Yann Gousseau, and Saïd Ladjal, "An Analysis of the Transfer Learning of Convolutional Neural Networks for Artistic Images," arXiv:2011.02727 [cs.CV], November 24, 2020, http://arxiv.org/abs/2011.02727.

46. Gonthier, Gousseau, and Ladjal, 8.

47. Robert Geirhos et al., "ImageNet-Trained CNNs Are Biased towards Texture; Increasing Shape Bias Improves Accuracy and Robustness," arXiv:1811.12231 [cs.CV], January 14, 2019, http://arxiv.org/abs/1811.12231.

48. Fabian Offert and Peter Bell, "Perceptual Bias and Technical Metapictures: Critical Machine Vision as a Humanities Challenge," *AI & Society* 36 (2021): 1133–1134.

49. Fabian Offert, "Images of Image Machines: Visual Interpretability in Computer Vision for Art," in *Computer Vision—ECCV 2018 Workshops*, ed. Laura Leal-Taixé and Stefan Roth (Cham, Switzerland: Springer, 2018), 3.

50. This point is certainly up for debate, as drapery has long been an important facet in the interpretation of Western art by art historians. Drapery can be a key component in iconographic analysis for Renaissance art, for example, particularly in biblical and devotional art in which color and style of drapery signifies the identity of the figure. For more on the significance of drapery for art history, see Anne Hollander, "The Fabric of Vision: The Role of Drapery in Art," *The Georgia Review* 29, no. 2 (1975): 414–465.

51. Offert, "Images of Image Machines," 4.

52. Mitra Azar, Geoff Cox, and Leonardo Impett, "Introduction: Ways of Machine Seeing," *AI & Society* 36 (2021): 1093–1104.

53. Stephen Cave, "The Problem with Intelligence: Its Value-Laden History and the Future of AI," in *Proceedings of the AAAI/ACM Conference on AI, Ethics, and Society, AIES '20* (New York: ACM, 2020), 29–35, https://doi.org/10.1145/3375627.3375813.

54. Offert and Bell, "Perceptual Bias and Technical Metapictures," 6.

55. Holm, "In Defense of the Black Box," 27.

56. Ella Hendriks and Shannon Hughes, "Van Gogh's Brushstrokes: Marks of Authenticity?," in *Art, Conservation and Authenticities; Material, Concept, Context*, ed. Erma Hermens and Tina Fiske (London: Archetype Publishing, 2009), 147; Elgammal, Kang, and Leeuw, "Picasso, Matisse, or a Fake?," 2.

57. Milton Esterow, "Art Experts Warn of a Surging Market in Fake Prints," *New York Times*, January 24, 2020, https://www.nytimes.com/2020/01/24/arts/design/fake-art-prints.html; Catherine Hickley, "A Museum Puts Its Fakes on Show," *New York Times*, September 30, 2020, https://www.nytimes.com/2020/09/30/arts/design/museum-ludwig-fakes-russian-avant-garde.html; Taylor Dafoe, "A London Court Has Upheld a Ruling Ordering an Art Collector to Pay Sotheby's $5.3 Million for Selling an Allegedly Forged Artwork," *Artnet News*, November 25, 2020, https://news.artnet.com/art-world/frans-hals-forgery-fairlight-1926818; Niraj Chokshi, "How Nuclear Bomb Tests Are Helping to Identify Art Forgeries," *New York Times*, June 6, 2019, https://www.nytimes.com/2019/06/06/arts/design/art-forgeries-atomic-nuclear-bomb.html; Christopher D. Shea, "Austrian Authorities Thwart Group Trying to Sell Fake Picassos," *New York Times*, November 8, 2016, https://www.nytimes.com/2016/11/09/arts/design/fake-picassos-austria-arrests.html; Colin Moynihan, "In Art Forgery Trial, Expert Witness Says Knoedler Gallery Relied on Fakes for Profit," *New York Times*, February 6, 2016, https://www.nytimes.com/2016/02/06/nyregion/in-art-forgery-trial-expert-witness-says-knoedler-gallery-relied-on-fakes-for-profit.html.

58. Gregory Day, "Explaining the Art Market's Thefts, Frauds, and Forgeries (and Why the Art Market Does Not Seem to Care)," *Vanderbilt Journal of Entertainment and Technology Law* 16, no. 3 (Spring 2014): 457–496.

59. Catherine Hickley, "Unknown or Unreal? The Shadow on Some Russian Avant-Garde Art," *New York Times*, April 6, 2018, https://www.nytimes.com/2018/04/06/arts/design/russian-avant-garde-art-forgery-disputes.html.

60. Roman Kräussl, Thorsten Lehnert, and Nicolas Martelin, "Is There a Bubble in the Art Market?," *Journal of Empirical Finance* 35 (January 1, 2016): 99–109; Tim Schneider, "Goodbye Art World, Hello Art Industry: How the Art Market Has Transformed—Radically—Over the Past 30 Years," *Artnet News*, November 25, 2019, https://news.artnet.com/market/how-the-art-world-became-the-art-industry-1710228.

61. Graham Bowley and Colin Moynihan, "Knoedler Gallery Heads to Trial in Sale of a Fake Rothko," *New York Times*, January 24, 2016, https://www.nytimes.com/2016/01/25/arts/design/knoedler-gallery-heads-to-trial-in-sale-of-a-fake-rothko.html; Anthony M. Amore, *The Art of the Con: The Most Notorious Fakes, Frauds, and Forgeries in the Art World* (New York: St. Martin's Griffin, 2015), 50.

62. Amore, *The Art of the Con*, 7.

63. Hickley, "Unknown or Unreal?"

64. Amore, *The Art of the Con*, 5.

65. Abraham Bredius, "A New Vermeer," *The Burlington Magazine for Connoisseurs* 71, no. 416 (1937): 211.

66. Lewis, *The Last Leonardo*, 39–40.

67. Ragai, *The Scientist and the Forger*, 8.

68. Carina Popovici, interview by Amanda Wasielewski, via email, April 1, 2021.

69. Art Recognition, accessed May 1, 2021, https://art-recognition.com/.

70. H. Jaap van den Herik and Eric O. Postma, "Discovering the Visual Signature of Painters," in *Future Directions for Intelligent Systems and Information Sciences*, ed. N. Kasabov (Heidelberg: Physica, 2000), 129–147; Igor Berezhnoy, Eric Postma, and Jaap van den Herik, "Computer Analysis of van Gogh's Complementary Colours," *Pattern Recognition Letters* 28, no. 6 (2007): 703–709; C. Richard Johnson et al., "Image Processing for Artist Identification," *IEEE Signal Processing Magazine* 25, no. 4 (July 2008): 37–48; N. van Noord, E. Hendriks, and E. Postma, "Toward Discovery of the Artist's Style: Learning to Recognize Artists by Their Artworks," *IEEE Signal Processing Magazine* 32, no. 4 (July 2015): 46–54; Nanne van Noord and Eric Postma, "Learning Scale-Variant and Scale-Invariant Features for Deep Image Classification," *Pattern Recognition* 61 (2017): 583–592.

71. Art Recognition.

72. Popovici, interview.

73. Art Recognition, "Technical Report: Computer Based Evaluation of Artwork Authenticity," June 19, 2020, https://art-recognition.com/request-a-sample-report/.

74. "New Tools Are Making It Easier to Authenticate Paintings," *Economist*, January 7, 2021, https://www.economist.com/books-and-arts/2021/01/07/new-tools-are-making-it-easier-to-authenticate-paintings.

75. Popovici, interview.

76. "New Tools Are Making It Easier to Authenticate Paintings."

77. Dalya Alberge, "Was Famed Samson and Delilah Really Painted by Rubens? No, Says AI," *The Observer*, September 26, 2021, https://www.theguardian.com/artanddesign/2021/sep/26/was-famed-samson-and-delilah-really-painted-by-rubens-no-says-ai.

78. Peter Bell and Fabian Offert, "Reflections on Connoisseurship and Computer Vision," *Journal of Art Historiography*, no. 24 (June 2021), https://arthistoriography.files.wordpress.com/2021/05/bell-offert.pdf, 2.

79. Art Trendex, accessed May 10, 2021, http://www.artrendex.com/.

80. Elgammal, Kang, and Leeuw, "Picasso, Matisse, or a Fake?"

81. M. M. van Dantzig, *Schilderkunst, maakwerk, vervalsching* (Amsterdam: H. J. Paris, 1937); M. M. van Dantzig, *Frans Hals, echt of onecht* (Amsterdam: H. J. Paris, 1937);

M. M. van Dantzig, *Johannes Vermeer, de "Emmausgangers" en de critici* (Leiden: Sijthoff, 1947); M. M. Van Dantzig, *Vincent? A New Method of Identifying the Artist and His Work and of Unmasking the Forger and His Products* (Amsterdam: Keesing, 1950); M. M. van Dantzig, *Pictology: An Analytical Method for Attribution and Evaluation of Pictures* (Leiden: Brill, 1973).

82. N. de Raadt, "Book Reviews: The Foundations of Pictology," *Synthesse* 11, no. 4 (December 1959): 395–400.

83. Johnson et al., "Image Processing for Artist Identification"; Hendriks and Hughes, "Van Gogh's Brushstrokes," 144; Noord, Hendriks, and Postma, "Toward Discovery of the Artist's Style"; Elgammal, Kang, and Leeuw, "Picasso, Matisse, or a Fake?"

84. Hendriks and Hughes, "Van Gogh's Brushstrokes," 147.

85. Johnson et al., "Image Processing for Artist Identification."

86. Andrew Dickson, "The New Tool in the Art of Spotting Forgeries: Artificial Intelligence," *Guardian*, August 6, 2018, http://www.theguardian.com/us-news/2018/aug/06/the-new-tool-in-the-art-of-spotting-forgeries-artificial-intelligence.

87. Elgammal, Kang, and Leeuw, "Picasso, Matisse, or a Fake?," 4.

88. Elgammal, Kang, and Leeuw, 4–5.

89. Amore, *The Art of the Con*, 9; "Over 50 Percent of Art Is Fake," *Artnet News*, October 13, 2014, https://news.artnet.com/market/over-50-percent-of-art-is-fake-130821.

90. Langmead et al., "Leonardo, Morelli, and the Computational Mirror," 7.

91. Langmead et al., 18.

92. Dickson, "The New Tool in the Art of Spotting Forgeries."

93. Diederik P. Kingma and Max Welling, "Auto-Encoding Variational Bayes," arXiv:1312.6114 [stat.ML], December 20, 2013, http://arxiv.org/abs/1312.6114v10; Ian Goodfellow et al., "Generative Adversarial Nets," in *Advances in Neural Information Processing Systems*, ed. Z. Ghahramani et al. (New York: Curran Associates, 2014), 2672–2680.

94. "DALL·E: Creating Images from Text," accessed July 25, 2022, https://openai.com/blog/dall-e/; Midjourney, accessed July 25, 2022, https://www.midjourney.com.

95. Tero Karras, Samuli Laine, and Timo Aila, "A Style-Based Generator Architecture for Generative Adversarial Networks," arXiv:1812.04948 [cs.NE], 2019, 4401–4410, https://doi.org/10.48550/arXiv.1812.04948.

96. Christopher Whyte, "Deepfake News: AI-Enabled Disinformation as a Multi-Level Public Policy Challenge," *Journal of Cyber Policy* 5, no. 2 (May 3, 2020): 199–217; Bryan C. Taylor, "Defending the State from Digital Deceit: The Reflexive Securitization of Deepfake," *Critical Studies in Media Communication* 38, no. 1 (January 1, 2021): 1–17.

97. Kristjan Kikerpill, "Choose Your Stars and Studs: The Rise of Deepfake Designer Porn," *Porn Studies* 7, no. 4 (October 1, 2020): 352–356; Chandell Gosse and Jacquelyn Burkell, "Politics and Porn: How News Media Characterizes Problems Presented by Deepfakes," *Critical Studies in Media Communication* 37, no. 5 (October 19, 2020): 497–511.

98. Next Rembrandt, accessed May 3, 2021, https://www.nextrembrandt.com/.

99. Jörg Marvin Gülzow, Liat Grayver, and Oliver Deussen, "Self-Improving Robotic Brushstroke Replication," *Arts* 7, no. 4 (December 2018).

100. Werner Schweibenz, "The Work of Art in the Age of Digital Reproduction," *Museum International* 70, no. 1–2 (January 1, 2018): 17; Jonathan Jones, "The Digital Rembrandt: A New Way to Mock Art, Made by Fools," *Guardian*, April 6, 2016, http://www.theguardian.com/artanddesign/jonathanjonesblog/2016/apr/06/digital-rembrandt-mock-art-fools; Peter Schjeldahl, "A Few Words about the Faux Rembrandt," *New Yorker*, April 8, 2016, https://www.newyorker.com/culture/culture-desk/a-few-words-about-the-faux-rembrandt.

101. Tsila Hassine and Ziv Neeman, "The Zombification of Art History: How AI Resurrects Dead Masters, and Perpetuates Historical Biases," *Journal of Science and Technology of the Arts* 11, no. 2 (May 1, 2019): 29.

102. Amore, *The Art of the Con.*

103. Luciano Floridi, "Artificial Intelligence, Deepfakes and a Future of Ectypes," *Philosophy & Technology* 31, no. 3 (September 1, 2018): 319.

104. Tim Schneider, "At Miami Art Week, Thousands of Works Created by Human Artists—And a Few by Artificial Intelligence, Too," *Artnet News*, December 7, 2018, https://news.artnet.com/exhibitions/aican-artificial-intelligence-scope-1412401; "Aican the AI Artist: Putting the Art in to Artificial Intelligence," *The Art Newspaper*, December 25, 2018, http://www.theartnewspaper.com/blog/feel-the-algo-rithm; Kevin Urgiles, "We Attended an AI's First Art Exhibit in NYC—Future Blink," Mashable, February 15, 2019, https://mashable.com/video/ai-art-exhibit-nyc/; Andrew Tarantola, "AICAN Doesn't Need Human Help to Paint like Picasso," Engadget, February 12, 2019, https://www.engadget.com/2019-02-12-aican-doesnt-need-human-help-to-paint-like-picasso.html; Ian Bogost, "The AI-Art Gold Rush Is Here," *Atlantic*, March 6, 2019, https://www.theatlantic.com/technology/archive/2019/03/ai-created-art-invades-chelsea-gallery-scene/584134/.

105. In addition to AICAN's being part of Artrendex, as mentioned, Obvious was listed as one of *Time*'s "Genius Companies of 2018" and has exhibited artworks as well as teamed up with brands like Nike for design projects. Gauthier Vernier and Pierre Fautrel, two of the members of Obvious, have a background in business, while the third, Hugo Caselles Dupré, is a computer engineer. "Obvious: The 50 Most Genius Companies of 2018," *Time*, accessed March 31, 2021, https://time.com/collection

/genius-companies-2018/5412644/obvious/; Michaela Cabrera, "The Artist as an Algorithm: Robot-Made Rembrandt for Sale," Reuters, September 22, 2018, https://www.reuters.com/article/us-france-art-artificial-intelligence-idUSKCN1M1222.

106. Cody Delistraty, "Trevor Paglen Is Putting the Art in Artificial Intelligence," *Wall Street Journal*, September 1, 2020, https://www.wsj.com/articles/trevor-paglen-art-artificial-intelligence-interview-11598963246.

107. Ian Cheng, "Bag of Beliefs," accessed February 2, 2022, http://iancheng.com/BOB.

108. Stephanie Dinkins, "Not the Only One," Stephanie Dinkins, accessed May 11, 2021, https://www.stephaniedinkins.com/ntoo.html.

109. Forensic Architecture, "Triple-Chaser," accessed May 10, 2021, https://forensic-architecture.org/investigation/triple-chaser.

110. Elizabeth A. Harris and Robin Pogrebin, "Warren Kanders Quits Whitney Board after Tear Gas Protests," *New York Times*, July 25, 2019, https://www.nytimes.com/2019/07/25/arts/whitney-warren-kanders-resigns.html.

111. James Vincent, "How Three French Students Used Borrowed Code to Put the First AI Portrait in Christie's," The Verge, October 23, 2018, https://www.theverge.com/2018/10/23/18013190/ai-art-portrait-auction-christies-belamy-obvious-robbie-barrat-gans.

112. Ciara Nugent, "How an Art Collective Is Using Artificial Intelligence to Make Paintings," *Time*, August 20, 2018, https://time.com/5357221/obvious-artificial-intelligence-art/.

113. Obvious, "Obvious, Explained," Medium, September 26, 2018, https://medium.com/@hello.obvious/ai-the-rise-of-a-new-art-movement-f6efe0a51f2e.

114. Jason Bailey, "Collective behind Christie's AI Art Tells All," Artnome, October 21, 2018, https://www.artnome.com/news/2018/10/13/collective-behind-christies-ai-art-tells-all.

115. Casey Quackenbush, "Painting Made by Artificial Intelligence Sells for $432,500," *Time*, October 26, 2018, https://time.com/5435683/artificial-intelligence-painting-christies/.

116. Joanna Zylinska, *AI Art: Machine Visions and Warped Dreams* (London: Open Humanities Press, 2020); Andreas Broeckmann, "The Machine as Artist as Myth," *Arts* 8, no. 1 (March 2019): 25; Aaron Hertzmann, "Can Computers Create Art?," *Arts* 7, no. 2 (June 2018): 18.

117. Bailey, "Collective behind Christie's AI Art Tells All."

118. HG Contemporary, "Faceless Portraits Transcending Time," accessed May 14, 2021, http://www.hgcontemporary.com/exhibitions/faceless-portraits-transcending-time.

119. Christie's, "Is Artificial Intelligence Set to Become Art's Next Medium?" accessed July 15, 2022, https://www.christies.com/features/a-collaboration-between-two-artists-one-human-one-a-machine-9332-1.aspx.

120. Bogost, "The AI-Art Gold Rush Is Here."

121. John Berger, *Portraits*, ed. Tom Overton (London: Verso, 2017), 10.

122. Antje Ehmann and Kodwo Eshun, "A to Z of HF or: 26 Introductions to HF," in *Harun Farocki: Against What? Against Whom?*, ed. Antje Ehmann and Kodwo Eshun (London: Koenig Books, 2009), 211; Harun Farocki, "Phantom Images," trans. Brian Poole, *Public* 29 (January 1, 2004): 17, https://public.journals.yorku.ca/index.php/public/article/view/30354.

123. Trevor Paglen, "Operational Images," *E-Flux Journal*, no. 59 (November 2014), https://www.e-flux.com/journal/59/61130/operational-images/.

124. Hito Steyerl, "In Defense of the Poor Image," *E-Flux Journal*, no. 10 (November 2009), https://www.e-flux.com/journal/10/61362/in-defense-of-the-poor-image/.

125. Steyerl, 1.

126. Steyerl, 8.

CHAPTER 3

1. David A. Mindell, *Digital Apollo: Human and Machine in Spaceflight* (Cambridge, MA: MIT Press, 2008).

2. "It's Man vs. Machine in 'Digital Apollo,'" "Talk of the Nation," NPR, July 3, 2008, https://www.npr.org/templates/story/story.php?storyId=92195902.

3. Michael Corris, "Systems Upgrade: Conceptual Art and the Recoding of Information, Knowledge and Technology," in *Proud to Be Flesh: A Mute Magazine Anthology of Cultural Politics after the Net*, ed. Josephine Berry Slater and Pauline van Mourik Broekman (London: Mute Publishing, 2009), 108.

4. György Buzsáki, *The Brain from Inside Out* (New York: Oxford University Press, 2019); Matthew Cobb, *The Idea of the Brain: The Past and Future of Neuroscience* (New York: Basic Books, 2020); Grace Lindsay, *Models of the Mind: How Physics, Engineering and Mathematics Have Shaped Our Understanding of the Brain* (London: Bloomsbury Sigma, 2021).

5. Andrew G. Ferguson, *The Rise of Big Data Policing: Surveillance, Race, and the Future of Law Enforcement* (New York: New York University Press, 2017), 123.

6. Nan Z. Da, "The Computational Case against Computational Literary Studies," *Critical Inquiry* 45, no. 3 (March 1, 2019): 601–639.

7. Brian Greenspan, "The Scandal of Digital Humanities," in *Debates in the Digital Humanities 2019* (Minneapolis: University of Minnesota Press, 2019), https://dhdebates.gc.cuny.edu/read/untitled-f2acf72c-a469-49d8-be35-67f9ac1e3a60/section/4b6be68c-802c-41f4-a2a5-284187ec0a5c#ch09.

8. Geoffrey Rockwell and Stéfan Sinclair, *Hermeneutica: Computer-Assisted Interpretation in the Humanities* (Cambridge, MA: MIT Press, 2016), 4.

9. Daniel Allington, Sarah Brouillette, and David Golumbia, "Neoliberal Tools (and Archives): A Political History of Digital Humanities," *Los Angeles Review of Books*, May 1, 2016, https://lareviewofbooks.org/article/neoliberal-tools-archives-political-history-digital-humanities/.

10. Allington, Brouillette, and Golumbia.

11. Tanya Clement, "An Information Science Question in DH Feminism," *Digital Humanities Quarterly* 9, no. 2 (September 2, 2015), 8.

12. Niall Atkinson et al., "Theses on Social Art History in the Age of Computational Methods," Humanities Commons, December 12, 2021, https://hcommons.org/deposits/item/hc:43511/, 16.

13. Adeline Koh, "A Letter to the Humanities: DH Will Not Save You," Hybrid Pedagogy, April 19, 2015, https://hybridpedagogy.org/a-letter-to-the-humanities-dh-will-not-save-you/.

14. James Elkins, *Six Stories from the End of Representation: Images in Painting, Photography, Astronomy, Microscopy, Particle Physics, and Quantum Mechanics, 1980–2000* (Stanford, CA: Stanford University Press, 2008); James Elkins, ed., *Visual Practices across the University* (Munich: Wilhelm Fink, 2007).

15. Elkins, *Six Stories from the End of Representation*, 14–16.

16. He cites Jonathan Crary's work as an example of this type of "evanescent" argumentation. Elkins, 9–11.

17. Elkins, 18.

18. Elkins, *Visual Practices across the University*, 8.

19. Elkins, *Six Stories from the End of Representation*, 17–18.

20. Reva Wolf, "The Shape of Time: Of Stars and Rainbows," *Art Journal* 68, no. 4 (December 1, 2009): 62–70; Reva Wolf, "Stars, Rainbows, and Living Dialects: George Kubler's Vision of History as Metaphor," *CES Contexto, Debates* 3 (September 2013): 29–40.

21. Wolf, "The Shape of Time," 35.

22. Elkins, *Visual Practices across the University*, 29–34.

23. Elkins, 50.

24. See Alan D. Sokal and Jean Bricmont, *Intellectual Impostures: Postmodern Philosophers' Abuse of Science* (London: Profile Books, 1998).

APPENDIX

1. B. Günsel, S. Sariel, and O. Icoglu, "Content-Based Access to Art Paintings," in *IEEE International Conference on Image Processing 2005*, vol. 2 (New York: IEEE, 2005), 558, doi: 10.1109/ICIP.2005.1530116.

2. Jana Zujovic et al., "Classifying Paintings by Artistic Genre: An Analysis of Features & Classifiers," in *2009 IEEE International Workshop on Multimedia Signal Processing* (New York: IEEE, 2009), 1–5, doi: 10.1109/MMSP.2009.5293271.

3. Behjat Siddiquie, Shiv N. Vitaladevuni, and Larry S. Davis, "Combining Multiple Kernels for Efficient Image Classification," in *2009 Workshop on Applications of Computer Vision (WACV)* (New York: IEEE, 2009), 1–8, https://doi.org/10.1109/WACV.2009.5403040.

4. Lior Shamir et al., "Impressionism, Expressionism, Surrealism: Automated Recognition of Painters and Schools of Art," *ACM Transactions on Applied Perception* 7, no. 2, article no. 8 (February 25, 2010): 1–17, https://doi.org/10.1145/1670671.1670672.

5. Mateja Čuljak et al., "Classification of Art Paintings by Genre," in *2011 Proceedings of the 34th International Convention MIPRO* (New York: IEEE, 2011), 1634–1639, https://ieeexplore.ieee.org/document/5967323.

6. Sergey Karayev et al., "Recognizing Image Style," arXiv:1311.3715 [cs.CV], November 15, 2013, https://doi.org/10.48550/arXiv.1311.3715.

7. Fahad Shahbaz Khan et al., "Painting-91: A Large Scale Database for Computational Painting Categorization," *Machine Vision and Applications* 25, no. 6 (August 1, 2014): 1385–1397.

8. Babak Saleh and Ahmed Elgammal, "Large-Scale Classification of Fine-Art Paintings: Learning the Right Metric on the Right Feature," arXiv:1505.00855 [cs.CV], May 5, 2015, https://arxiv.org/abs/1505.00855; Babak Saleh and Ahmed Elgammal, "Large-Scale Classification of Fine-Art Paintings: Learning the Right Metric on the Right Feature," *International Journal for Digital Art History*, no. 2 (October 18, 2016): 70–93.

9. Yaniv Bar, Noga Levy, and Lior Wolf, "Classification of Artistic Styles Using Binarized Features Derived from a Deep Neural Network," in *Computer Vision—ECCV 2014 Workshops*, ed. Lourdes Agapito, Michael M. Bronstein, and Carsten Rother, Lecture Notes in Computer Science (Cham, Switzerland: Springer, 2015), 71–84, https://doi.org/10.1007/978-3-319-16178-5_5.

10. Wei Ren Tan et al., "Ceci n'est pas une pipe: A Deep Convolutional Network for Fine-Art Paintings Classification," in *2016 IEEE International Conference on Image Processing (ICIP)* (New York: IEEE, 2016), 3703–3707, https://doi.org/10.1109/ICIP.2016.7533051.

11. Hui Mao, Ming Cheung, and James She, "DeepArt: Learning Joint Representations of Visual Arts," in *Proceedings of the 25th ACM International Conference on Multimedia* (New York: ACM, 2017), 1183–1191, https://doi.org/10.1145/3123266.3123405.

12. Ahmed Elgammal et al., "The Shape of Art History in the Eyes of the Machine," arXiv:1801.07729 [cs.AI], January 23, 2018, http://arxiv.org/abs/1801.07729v2.

13. Noa Garcia and George Vogiatzis, "How to Read Paintings: Semantic Art Understanding with Multi-Modal Retrieval," arXiv:1810.09617 [cs.CV], October 22, 2018, http://arxiv.org/abs/1810.09617.

14. Gjorgji Strezoski and Marcel Worring, "OmniArt: A Large-Scale Artistic Benchmark," *ACM Transactions on Multimedia Computing, Communications, and Applications* 14, no. 4, article no. 88 (October 23, 2018): 1–21, https://doi.org/10.1145/3273022.

15. Eren Gultepe, Thomas Edward Conturo, and Masoud Makrehchi, "Predicting and Grouping Digitized Paintings by Style Using Unsupervised Feature Learning," *Journal of Cultural Heritage* 31 (May 1, 2018): 13–23.

16. Eva Cetinic, Tomislav Lipic, and Sonja Grgic, "A Deep Learning Perspective on Beauty, Sentiment, and Remembrance of Art," *IEEE Access* 7 (2019): 73694–73710, https://doi.org/10.1109/ACCESS.2019.2921101.

17. Catherine Sandoval, Elena Pirogova, and Margaret Lech, "Two-Stage Deep Learning Approach to the Classification of Fine-Art Paintings," *IEEE Access* 7 (2019): 41770–41781.

18. Corneliu Florea, Cosmin Toca, and Fabian Gieseke, "Artistic Movement Recognition by Boosted Fusion of Color Structure and Topographic Description," in *2017 IEEE Winter Conference on Applications of Computer Vision (WACV)* (New York: IEEE, 2017), 569–577.

19. Liyi Chen and Jufeng Yang, "Recognizing the Style of Visual Arts via Adaptive Cross-Layer Correlation," in *Proceedings of the 27th ACM International Conference on Multimedia, MM '19* (New York: ACM, 2019), 2459–2467, https://doi.org/10.1145/3343031.3350977.

20. Jipeng Gao, Haolin Zhou, and Yicheng Zhang, "The Performance of Two CNN Methods in Artworks Aesthetic Feature Recognition," in *Proceedings of the 2020 12th International Conference on Machine Learning and Computing, ICMLC 2020* (New York: ACM, 2020), 289–296, https://doi.org/10.1145/3383972.3383974.

21. Sheng-hua Zhong, Xingsheng Huang, and Zhijiao Xiao, "Fine-Art Painting Classification via Two-Channel Dual Path Networks," *International Journal of Machine Learning*

and Cybernetics 11, no. 1 (January 1, 2020): 137–152, https://doi.org/10.1007/s13042-019-00963-0.

22. Cheikh Brahim El Vaigh et al., "GCNBoost: Artwork Classification by Label Propagation through a Knowledge Graph," arXiv:2105.11852 [cs.LG], May 25, 2021, http://arxiv.org/abs/2105.11852.

23. Garcia and Vogiatzis, "How to Read Paintings."

24. Benjamin Renoust et al., "Historical and Modern Features for Buddha Statue Classification," arXiv:1909.12921 [cs.CV], October 6, 2019, http://arxiv.org/abs/1909.12921.

25. Giovanna Castellano, Giovanni Sansaro, and Gennaro Vessio, "Integrating Contextual Knowledge to Visual Features for Fine Art Classification," arXiv:2105.15028v2 [cs.CV], September 28, 2021, http://arxiv.org/abs/2105.15028.

26. Giovanna Castellano and Gennaro Vessio, "Deep Learning Approaches to Pattern Extraction and Recognition in Paintings and Drawings: An Overview," *Neural Computing and Applications* 33, no. 19 (October 1, 2021): 12263–12282.

27. Wentao Zhao et al., "How to Represent Paintings: A Painting Classification Using Artistic Comments," *Sensors* 21, no. 6 (January 2021): 1940, https://doi.org/10.3390/s21061940.

28. Wentao Zhao et al., "Compare the Performance of the Models in Art Classification," *PLOS One* 16, no. 3 (March 12, 2021): e0248414, https://doi.org/10.1371/journal.pone.0248414.

Index

Note: Page numbers in *italics* indicate figures.